The Complete Idiot's Reference Card

The Top Ten Tips for Winning Back Your Time

1. Leave the office or your workplace on time at least several workdays per week, having accomplished what you sought to accomplish *within a normal workday*.

2. Watch less television; cruise the Internet less.

3. Pay others to do tasks you don't want to do so you're free to address more important stuff; break the cycle of spending for items that don't free up your time and then having to work harder to pay bills.

4. Recognize that while nobody loves filing, hereafter it's essential to staying in control.

5. Buy any device *you can easily master* that you believe will make you more efficient.

6. Get into the habit of doing one thing at a time. Stop doubling up on activities such as reading the paper on a treadmill.

7. Get a solid night's sleep (eight hours for most adults) at least five to seven times a week.

8. Enter the "wholesale throwout" business—throw out accumulating piles of newspapers, magazines, and reports that offer little to your career and life.

9. Earmark several hours each week during which you'll take in no new information and have nothing to read or do (especially Saturdays and Sundays).

10. Read this book; pick some changes to make. Incorporate each one slowly and thoroughly; let it sink in, then move to the next.

Five of the Worst Mistakes People Make with Their Time

➤ Spending time on concerns that are not chosen priorities.

➤ Underestimating the time that tasks or activities will actually consume.

➤ Allowing too many interruptions.

➤ Saying "yes" too frequently to requests for their time.

➤ Not getting help.

Five Unbelievable-but-True Facts About Your Time

➤ You're likely to live longer than you think you will—perhaps ten or more years longer.

➤ Anything you do for an average of 30 minutes each day (equal to over 180 hours for 365 days) consumes *a full week's time for every year of your life.*

➤ You're likely to spend eight years of your life watching electronically how other people (supposedly) live.

➤ You're working about 360 hours more annually (equal to nine 40-hour work weeks) than people in Germany.

➤ You may be engaging in 10-to-15-second bouts of "microsleep" while driving your car!

alpha books

Five Ways to Feel Better by the End of Each Workday

➤ Don't put anything more on *today's* to-do list late in the day.
➤ Tackle the issues you face in *descending* order of importance.
➤ Work on one thing at a time.
➤ Pause periodically, if briefly, throughout the day.
➤ Acknowledge yourself for what you *did* accomplish.

Time "Slows Down" and You Seem to Have More When...

➤ You close your eyes for one full minute and imagine a pleasant scene.
➤ You delete three non-essential items from your to-do list *without* doing them.
➤ You clear your desk of everything except the primary task.

Time "Speeds Up" and You Seem to Have Less When...

➤ You take in more information than you can absorb.
➤ You work in front of a clock to meet an unrealistic time-frame.
➤ You jam-pack your calendar with activities and appointments.

Hold That Thought!

➤ You are not your tasks; you are not your job; you are not your title.
➤ Some people are late bloomers; James Michener wrote his first book at age 42 and wrote books for over 40 more years.
➤ Most millionaires make their first million slowly, over many years.
➤ You'll never be younger than you are right now.

Try These to Catch Up with This Week!

➤ Telecommute at least once a week.
➤ Get dressed each morning quietly, sans radio or TV.
➤ Do something fun once a week on the way home from work.
➤ Regard each piece of paper entering your "personal kingdom" as a likely traitor.
➤ Make a lunch date with a friend, not a coworker or client.

You Know You're Winning Back Your Time When...

➤ You leave home in the morning with grace and ease.
➤ You enjoy a leisurely lunch.
➤ You often depart from the workplace at normal closing hours—and feel fine about it.
➤ You stay in shape and at your desired weight.
➤ You have time to be with and enjoy friends and relatives.

The COMPLETE IDIOT'S GUIDE TO

Managing Your Time

by Jeff Davidson, MBA, CMC

alpha books

A Division of Macmillan General Reference
A Pearson Education Macmillan Company
201 W. 103rd Street, Indianapolis, IN 46290

To my wonderful family—past and future—who support me in the use of my time, practically all the time.

©1995 by Jeff Davidson, MBA, CMC

International Standard Book Number: 0-02-863801-8
Library of Congress Catalog Card Number is available upon request from the publisher.

02 01 00 99   4 3 2 1

Interpretation of the printing code: the rightmost number of the first series of numbers is the year of the book's printing; the rightmost number of the second series of numbers is the number of the book's printing. For example, a printing code of 99-1 shows that the first printing of the book occurred in 1999.

Printed in the United States of America

Publisher
Theresa H. Murtha

Associate Publisher
Lisa A. Bucki

Production Editor
Barry Childs-Helton

Imprint Manager
Kelly Dobbs

Designer
Kim Scott

Illustrator
Judd Winick

Indexer
Christopher Cleveland

Production Team
*Heather Butler, Angela Calvert, Kim Cofer, David Garratt
Erika Millen, Beth Rago, Erich Richter, Christine Tyner*

*Special thanks to Claire Conway and Carol Krucoff for ensuring the
technical accuracy of this book.*

Contents at a Glance

Contents

9   I Can, Therefore It's Asked of Me, or (Worse) I Volunteer!   91

10   Whipping Your Office into Shape   101

Foreword

You'd think that after all these years and all the time-management books published, most professionals would be adept at most aspects of self-management. Yet you have only to look around your own office and organization to see that just the reverse is happening. People today seem less able to keep pace, less integrated, and less effective as self-managers.

Given all that has happened in the last couple of decades, it's not so surprising. Each of us faces the specter of ever-increasing change. Often a new piece of technology that enters our lives means more instructions to learn, instituting a whole new way of doing things. Change itself seems to occur at an accelerating pace.

In this breakthrough book, Jeff Davidson offers a plan with which you can consistently *win back* control of your time, despite the rigors of trying to flourish in an ever-changing society.

Jeff wrote this book with the specific intention of giving you hands-on, highly practical solutions to the day-to-day problems you face. Everything in the book is presented in an honest, down-to-earth, and often amusing way. I found myself smiling and nodding in agreement all the way through.

Its basic truths run from page to page. Jeff starts with the basic premise that to win back your time you need to develop, or redevelop, the habit of leaving your workplace at the normal closing hour—if at first only one day a week, and then two days, and then three days, and then nearly every day. He follows with nineteen more chapters, just as compelling, that address various aspects of winning back your time at work and in your life in general. He concludes with the message that the best is yet to come, and convincingly tells us why this is so.

Not just another treatise on applying antiquated time-management rules, this is a book of guiding principles; ultimately this book is a gift to career-minded professionals everywhere who know that the quality of their lives, for the rest of their lives, depends upon how they approach each day—starting with this day.

The suggestions that Jeff offers don't require an upheaval in the way you work or live; most can be implemented naturally and easily. Indeed, Jeff believes that any change representing a radical departure from what you already do will fail more often than not. He has presented his suggestions with great care, recognizing that you already have more than enough to do.

Nearly all of what Jeff recommends can be woven into the tapestry of your life as it exists now. Consequently, this is a book you'll want to keep nearby and refer to often. Depending on the specifics of your situation, many chapters and many passages will merit multiple readings.

At the end of each chapter, as is customary in this Macmillan series, Jeff concisely presents "the least you need to know" from that chapter. If you only follow those three or four suggestions, you'll do just fine.

I am enthusiastic about the results you can achieve in reading and following the ideas in this book. As you find yourself winning back more and more of your time, please do others around you the ultimate favor—share the principles in this book with them so that they, too, can win back their time.

Dr. Janet Lapp

Noted San Diego-based consultant and trainer in the topic of change—personal, professional, and corporate—and publisher of *The Change Letter*.

Introduction: Change Without (Well, with Hardly Any!) Pain

This is a book about winning back your time. The chances are astronomical-to-nearly-100% that you lost it over the last several years. The quest to *win back* your time is a noble pursuit, but it's a fast-paced and frenzied existence you're enduring. With all that competes for your time and attention, how do you alter the pace of your career and life so *you* are in control of your time? How can you enjoy what your career and life have to offer, and once again have time to reflect, to ponder, to muse?

Let's explore how to improve the quality of your life for the rest of your life. Whoa! To achieve all this, first understand that whatever changes you make have to come *without* too much pain. I know this is contrary to what you've been led to believe about change, but bear with me. If the changes needed to win back your time are too difficult—too many rules, too many things to remember or do—then you're not going to stay with them.

Instead, the steps need to be simpler—a moderate shift here, an adjustment there. Gradual, subtle, natural changes in what you're already doing yield far greater long-term results. Changes that are radical or anxiety-provoking have much less chance of taking hold. Why? Well, if you've been alive for 25, 35, 45 years or more, it took that long to become who you are—just the way you are. You're clearly perfect at it! You're probably not going to change suddenly in 35 minutes or 35 hours, and in many cases not in 35 days.

If the changes you undertake are too painful or too upsetting *to your current ways of doing things,* they won't last—or be effective. *Ignore* anything in this book that represents too much of a stretch for you right now. Proceed with the suggestions you can undertake most readily. As you initiate more changes, others will fall into place from the momentum of your actions. Such a deal! Gradually, with the proper perspective, a few specific techniques, and some built-in follow-up, you'll be able to win back your time naturally and easily.

I've structured the book to ease you into each topic as you reclaim your time. We'll move from broad-based to nitty-gritty workaday issues; in the last few chapters, we tackle personal perspectives.

Part 1, "This Is How Much Time You Get," looks at the broad context of why you feel mounting time pressure, and offers specific strategies for winning back your time—starting with the fundamental notion of leaving work at a semi-decent hour *and feeling good about it!* You'll get a look at some specific ways your time is depleted, why many others face the same predicament you do, and how to exert more control over where your time goes. I'll discuss how you can determine what's most important to you and what will be required (realistically) to support your priorities.

Part 2, "Taking Charge of Your Turf," focuses on specific areas of your life—including how much sleep you're getting (versus how much you *need*), responding to the requests others make for your time, keeping your office organized, mastering your own files, and handling correspondence efficiently. You'll find tools and technologies that can help you be more efficient or (if you don't use them) slide farther into the morass of the overwhelmed.

Part 3, "Thinking Your Way Around Time Traps," discusses key areas for saving time—making decisions more quickly, honing the ability to focus on *one thing at a time*, and the importance of *constantly reducing what you hold on to* (it'll keep your own systems uncomplicated).

Part 4, "Peace-of-Mind Goals," delves into higher-order notions such as undertaking a quest to live in "Real Time," catching up with today, and occasionally withdrawing from the maddening crowd.

I conclude with an observation about why the best is yet to come—assuming, of course, that you *follow* the sage advice offered throughout! I suggest pausing after each chapter and *acting on some of what you've taken in*—otherwise you're unlikely to act on anything in the book. Tackle that "human nature" if you want your time back!

Extras

I have used some special boxed notes throughout the book to help you learn just what you need. These include:

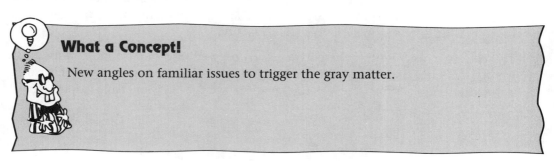

What a Concept!

New angles on familiar issues to trigger the gray matter.

Warning
Pitfalls to avoid as you win back your time.

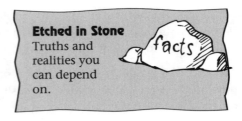

Etched in Stone
Truths and realities you can depend on.

Word Power
New words and terms that can help you know what to look for.

Go!
Actions to take right away, while you're thinking about it.

To start right away, flip to Chapter 1 for a look at the reality of how much time you get in this life. (If you're lucky, that is!) Otherwise let's roll some credits...

Acknowledgments

Thanks to all the wonderful folks at Macmillan General Reference for picking me to write this book and giving me the support that would make it the winner that it is! Thanks to Theresa Murtha, Lisa Bucki, Jen Perillo, and Barry Childs-Helton for their careful editing, insights, and guidance.

Thanks to the folks in marketing, sales, and promotion for ensuring that people throughout the world will be exposed to this book. I'd also like to thank my agent, Trent Price, for his unceasing efforts in making this book a reality.

Thanks also to Cole Ruth for extensive, expert copy-editing and proofing, Julie Christi Crain for her insightful copy-editing, Sandy Knudsen for her fingers that fly over the keyboard like quicksilver, and Valerie Davidson, age 5, who is my daily inspiration.

Special Thanks to the Technical Reviewers...

The Complete Idiot's Guide to Managing Your Time was reviewed by experts who not only checked the technical accuracy of what you'll learn here, but also provided insight and guidance to help us ensure that this book gives you everything you need to know to begin making better decisions about how you spend your time. We extend our special thanks to these folks:

Claire Conway is a freelance writer who served as features editor for *Psychology Today* in New York City. Prior to that, she was managing editor of *Stanford Medicine* magazine, a publication of the Stanford University Medical School Alumni Association. Born and raised in California, she received an M.S.J. from Northwestern's Medill School of Journalism.

Carol Krucoff a health and fitness column for the *Washington Post*, where she was founding editor of the weekly Health Section. A freelance writer based in Chapel Hill, North Carolina, she contributes to a variety of publications, including *Reader's Digest*, *Self*, *Parents*, and *The Saturday Evening Post*. She also teaches Creative Nonfiction for Duke University's Continuing Education Department. She has two school-age children, is married to a cardiologist, and holds a brown belt in karate.

Trademarks

All terms mentioned in this book that are known to be trademarks or servicemarks are listed here. In addition, terms suspected of being trademarks or servicemarks have been appropriately capitalized.

Fortune Company Profiles is a trademark of Avenue Technologies, Inc.

HeadsUp is a trademark of Individual, Inc.

LEXIS and NEXIS are trademarks of Mead Data Central.

Mac is a trademark of Apple Computer.

Microsoft Net and Microsoft Windows are trademarks of Microsoft Corporation.

Netscape is a trademark of Netscape Communications, Inc.

Post-It is a trademark of 3M Company.

Research Reports is a trademark of Standard and Poor.

Turbo Tax and Quicken are trademarks of InTuit, Inc.

WESTfax is a trademark of Westlaw.

WinFax Pro and FaxPro are trademarks of Delrina Technology, Inc.

Part 1
This Is How Much Time You Get

Ah, life! For all that's written about life, it is still finite. Your life, in particular, had a distinct beginning and will have a distinct ending—at least the part that occurs on earth—unless, of course, you believe you're coming back as someone else or in some other form. In that case (cosmically speaking), you're not facing any time-pressure and might not need this book—whatever you don't take care of in this life, you can always address in your next life, or in the second or third life after this one. Of course, advances in human technology are making the future more complex all the time; you'll have a whole new set of challenges if you come back as a human being. (You know, come to think of it, maybe you are better off continuing with this book now. If you learn to win back your time in this life, you'll have a head start in future lives….)

Ahem…back in the here-and-now, I'll gently present seven hard-hitting chapters that explore some mysteries of the ages. Among these revelations: why staying longer can be self-defeating, what really happens to your time, quality (versus quantity) of life, whose fault the present mess isn't, getting real and getting what you want, identifying and going after your priorities, and why time and money are not the same thing. You know…the basics…

I'll Just Stay a Bit Longer This Evening to Finish Everything

In This Chapter

➤ The essential step to win back your time is right there before you!

➤ Make changes that are easy to put in place and to follow

➤ A dynamic bargain: feel good about what you've done—and about leaving

➤ Many ways to leave on time; choose a few and they'll work

We begin at the beginning, logically enough. One of the worst time traps you can possibly fall into is believing that by working a little longer (or taking work home on the weekend) you can finally "catch up." This is a fallacy that will keep you perpetually chasing the clock for at least the rest of your career, and maybe the rest of your life.

Hey! I sympathize with you if you've been caught in the trap of working longer or taking work home with you. At face value, these maneuvers probably seem a logical response to pressures you face. For too many people, they are also a trap.

The Erroneous Notion of Staying Longer

If you find yourself perpetually taking work home or working a little longer at the office, these actions become the norm. Soon you're taking another thirty or forty pages of reading material home at night as if this habit were *simply the way it is.*

What a Concept!

Yes, *on occasion* it makes sense to take work home from the office. All career achievers do. During specific campaigns (like the launch of a new business, product, or service), when you change jobs, or when you're approaching a significant event, it makes sense to bone up and spend a few extra hours at work. These practices, however, need to be the exception—not the rule.

When you consistently work longer hours or take work home from the office, you begin to forget what it's like to have a free weeknight—and eventually a free weekend. I've observed the working styles of some of the most successful people in America—multimillionaires, best-selling authors, high-powered corporate executives, association leaders, top-level government officials, educators—people from all walks of life. The most successful people in any endeavor maintain a healthy balance between their work and non-work lives.

Americans are working more, *but not everybody does it this way.* The typical German worker, by comparison, works 320 to 400 *fewer* hours per year than his American counterpart. A journalist for *U.S. News and World Report* observed that Europeans are shocked to discover that most Americans get *only two weeks* of annual vacation time. The norm in Germany (as well as France and Great Britain) is five weeks off annually. Entrepreneurs, as a whole, work the longest—an average of 54 hours a week, if you can believe they're honest in reporting their true work time (they probably work many *more* hours than they reported).

Warning

Department of Labor statistics reveal that in the past two dozen years, the amount of time Americans have spent at their jobs has risen steadily.

Americans also are sleeping less (the subject of Chapter 8), which significantly affects work performance. In fact, all aspects of life are becoming more complex. As a result, you may be enjoying your life a bit less these days (Chapter 3 discusses five mega-realities that may tell you why).

People aren't just working more and running around more because they feel like it. Our society as a whole has become more competitive and demanding. Employers require more. Kids have to be a part of more activities. There are kabillions of entertainment options. So we work more hours, try to keep up, quietly go nuts, and consider it normal.

What if You're a Student, Homemaker, or Part-Time Worker?

Alas, you get no break in this world. Nearly all of the time-pressure problems that plague denizens of the full-time working world will visit you as well. While you may have extra moments to yourself here and there, *everyone* who holds any position of responsibility today—and that includes studying, managing a home, or caring for others—faces pressures unknown to previous generations (as you'll learn in Chapter 3).

Your key to reducing the time pressure you feel (and a recurring theme throughout this book) is that you don't need to stay longer at your work—or workplace. Indeed, to reclaim your day you *cannot* stay longer.

What a Concept!

Your quest becomes accomplishing that which you seek to accomplish *within* the eight or nine hours you call the workday.

Workdays—Like Careers and Lives—Are Finite

Suppose your workday is 8:00 a.m. to 5:00 p.m. with an hour for lunch, yielding a total working time of eight hours. Study after study shows that most people are only working about sixty percent of those eight hours for which they were hired. Even in these downsizing times, most people work a daily average of only four hours and forty-eight minutes on the tasks, responsibilities, and activities for which they were hired. Notable exceptions include the self-employed and the fanatically driven.

Many people don't work a full eight hours a day—even though they spend eight hours on the job—as these charts illustrate.

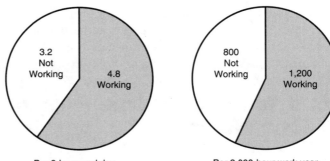

Per 8-hour workday.   Per 2,000-hour work year.

Okay, okay. So you're not among those who dawdle and you certainly don't goof off for forty percent of your day. Still, it's unlikely that you're working the solid eight hours. Among the many factors that inhibit your inclination to work a solid eight hours every day are:

1. **Too many domestic tasks.** See Chapter 7 to learn how easy it is to get stuck thinking that if you spend a few minutes here and a few minutes there, taking care of domestic tasks yourself, you can stay on top of it all, save a little money, and cruise into work in high gear.

2. **Not getting enough sleep.** See Chapter 8, which discusses why you're probably not getting enough sleep, and how this leads to lack of efficiency and effectiveness. Zzzz.

3. **Overcommitting.** See Chapter 9 about how widely available technology gives managers and businesses the opportunity to get more done—and also to expect more from their employees. Much more.

4. **Not being sufficiently organized.** See Chapter 10, which explains that a desk is not a filing cabinet, and window sills and the corners of your room are not permanent storage locations. You can rule an empire from a desk, if you know how to do it correctly.

5. **Lacking effective tools.** See Chapter 12 on how you can put new technology to work for you—and how to avoid being overwhelmed by what you acquire.

In addition to these factors, over-socializing is the norm in many offices. Among some professionals, rituals such as sharpening three pencils, refilling the coffee cup, making a personal call, or waiting until the clock on the wall is at the top of the hour have to occur before they get down to work. (I know, that's not you, but some people do this.)

2,000 Hours a Year Is a Lot

Eight-hour workdays, of which you have 250 a year, yield a work year of 2000 hours. Can you get done in 2,000 hours that which you want to do (or for which you were hired)? Yes! Two thousand hours, 200 hours, eight hours, even one hour, can be a great deal of time if you have the mindset, the quiet, and the tools you need to be productive.

The Discipline (and Habit) of Leaving and Feeling Good About It

To sustain the habit of leaving work on time, start with a small step. For example, decide that on every Tuesday you will stop working on time and take no extra work home with you. After freeing up Tuesdays for an entire month, perhaps add Thursdays. In another month, add Mondays; in the fourth month, add Wednesdays. I'm assuming there's no way you work late on Friday! (Or *do* you? If you do, then start with Fridays!)

What transpires in the first month when you've decided that each Tuesday will be a normal eight- or nine-hour workday and nothing more? Automatically you begin to be more focused about what you want to get done on Tuesdays. Almost imperceptibly, you begin to parcel out your time during the day more judiciously.

By midday, stop and assess what you've done and what else you'd like to get done. Near the end of the day, assess what more you can (*realistically*) get done, and what's best to leave for subsequent days.

You begin to set a natural, internal alignment in motion. Your internal cylinders fire in harmony with what it takes for you to have a buoyant, productive workday on Tuesday and leave on time.

Warning
Take away any of these crucial elements—come to work feeling exhausted, keep getting interrupted, or be mentally unprepared to give your all—and one hour, eight hours, 200 hours, 2000 hours, or more won't be sufficient for you to do your work. (See Chapter 15 for a neat system to minimize interruptions.)

What a Concept!

For some reason that only the gods of Mount Olympus can explain, once you've solidly made the decision to leave on time on Tuesdays, every cell in your body works in unison to help you accomplish your proclamation.

Anticipating the Unexpected; Establishing Boundaries

By now you're probably thinking that these perspectives may look good on paper, but what about when the boss comes in and hands you a four-inch stack at 3:45 in the afternoon? Or what about when you get a fax, an e-mail message, or another message that upsets the applecart? These things *do* happen. Take a real-world approach to your time, your life, and what you're likely to face during the typical workday. Consider how to approach the predictable impediments to leaving on time on Tuesday.

Rather than treat an unexpected project that gets dumped in your lap late in the day as an intrusion, stretch a tad to view it as something else. You got the project because you were trusted, accomplished, or in some cases, simply there.

Many government workers have no trouble establishing their time boundaries at work. They leave on time because that's what their government policy manual says, right there in clause 92-513-ak7-1, subclause 8-PD 601-00 07, paragraph 6.12, line 8—*no overtime, pal*. If you're in the private sector, however, you may not have such regulations on your side. (See Chapter 9 for some options you *do* have.)

If you're concerned that staying late and putting in ridiculous hours is *de rigueur* in your organizational culture, you need data and special strategies. First the data! Professor Carey Cooper, an American at Manchester University in England, is one of Europe's foremost stress specialists. He has found that *performance declines by 25 percent* after a sixty-hour workweek. He also has calculated that the annual cost of stress-related illnesses attributed to overwork tops $80 billion in the U.S.—more than $1600 a year for every other worker in America. Other studies show that work output is growing faster in Germany than in the U.S.—even though (as you've seen) Germans work fewer hours than Americans.

Stated bluntly, excess work hours put in by already-overtaxed employees *are of negative value* to an organization when viewed in the context of overall work performance, direct health-care costs, and productivity lost to absenteeism and general lethargy on the job.

Now the strategies:

1. Let it be known that you maintain a home office where you devote *countless* hours to the organization after 5:00 each evening. Then take most evenings off.

2. Invite bosses and coworkers to your home for some other reason and conveniently give them a tour of your command-center-away-from-the-office.

3. When you discuss your work, focus on the *results* you achieve (as opposed to the hours you log after 5:00). It is exceedingly difficult for anyone to argue with results.

4. Find the best role-models of outstanding achievers within your organization who leave at (or close to) normal closing time at least a few nights a week; drop hints about the role-models' working styles in conversation with others in your organization.

5. Acquire whatever tools of technology (see Chapter 12) will help you to be more productive. If your organization won't foot the bill, do it yourself. Often your long-term output and advancement will more than offset the upfront cost.

6. On those evenings you do work late at the office, be conspicuous. Make the rounds; let yourself be seen.

7. On those evenings when you take work home, use oversize containers or boxes to transport your projects. In fact, bring boxes back and forth to the office even when you have no intention of doing any work at home.

8. If zipping out at 5:00 carries a particular stigma in your office, leave earlier. Huh? Yes, schedule an appointment across town for 3:30 p.m. and when it's over, *don't* head back to the office. This is a tried-and-true strategy for laggards *but it can work just as well for highly productive types like you.* If you feel guilty, work for the last 30 or 45 minutes at home.

Right now I'm only talking about ending work at a sane hour *one* night a week. If this represents too much of a leap for you, either stop reading this book and continue suffering the way you have been, or change jobs and try to find a more enlightened employer. Otherwise begin to plot your strategy now—it's your job and it's your life.

What About Those Sly Devils at Places Like Microsoft?

On the way to developing Microsoft Windows 95 and getting it out the darn door on time, the elite Seattle nerd corps found themselves working progressively longer hours each day. For some, it became unbearable. Some went into a robot phase (you know—work, work, work, work…). Some quit. Some will be added to the ranks of the millionaires. All got the opportunity to chill out afterward. Yes, there are excruciatingly tough campaigns, but they are of *finite* duration.

Crunch times come and go. You don't want to get into the bind of treating the typical workday like crunch time. Then you start to do foolish things like throwing your time at challenges instead of devising less time-consuming ways to handle them—all of which equates to not leaving on time next Thursday.

> **Etched in Stone**
> In the short run, anyone can be a victim, even you. In the long run, there are no victims—only willing participants.

Striking a Dynamic Bargain with Yourself

A master stroke for winning back your time at any point in your day, Tuesdays or any other day, is to continually strike a *dynamic bargain* with yourself. It's a self-reinforcing tool for achieving a desired outcome that you've identified within a certain time-frame, as in the end of the day!

Suppose it's 2:15 and there are three more items you'd like to accomplish before the day is over. Here's the magic phrase I want you to begin using:

"What would it take for me to feel good about ending work on time today?"

I have this phrase as a poster on my wall in my office. This phrase is powerful. It gives you the freedom to feel good about leaving the office on time because you struck the dynamic bargain with yourself *wherein you said exactly what you needed to accomplish to feel good about leaving on time that day*.

Word Power
The **dynamic bargain** mentioned here is an agreement you make with yourself to assess what you've accomplished (and what more you want to accomplish) from time to time throughout the day—adjusting to new conditions as they emerge.

Suppose you have three items on your plate that you want to finish so you can feel good about leaving on time. Then the boss drops a bomb on your desk late in the day. You automatically get to strike a *new* dynamic bargain with yourself, given the prevailing circumstances. Your new bargain may include simply making sufficient headway on the project that's been dropped in your lap, or accomplishing two of your previous tasks and *X* percent of this new project.

At the End of the Week, Feel Good About What You've Done

The same principle holds true for leaving the office on Friday: feeling good about what you accomplished during the workweek. Here is the question to ask yourself (usually sometime around midday on Friday, but often as early as Thursday):

"By the end of work on Friday, what do I want to have accomplished so I can feel good about the weekend?"

By employing such questions and striking these dynamic bargains with yourself, you get to avoid what too many professionals in society still confront: leaving, on most workdays, not feeling good about what they've accomplished, not having a sense of completion, and bringing work home. If you're like most of these people, you want to be more productive. You want to get raises and promotions, but you don't want to have a lousy life in the process!

Rather than striking dynamic bargains with themselves, most people frequently do the opposite. They had several things they wanted to accomplish that day—and did, in fact, accomplish some of them, crossing them off the list. Then, *to make sure it would be another day they left their offices feeling beat up about what they had yet to do, they added several more items to the list.* On top of the impediments imposed by others, here you have the perfect prescription for leaving the workplace every day *not feeling good* about what you've accomplished: always having a lengthy, running list of "stuff" you have to do, and never getting any sense of being in control of your time.

Go!
Regardless of projects, e-mail, faxes, or other intrusions into your perfect world, *continually* strike that dynamic bargain with yourself so you get to leave the workplace on time, feeling good about what you accomplished.

A Self-Reinforcing Process

When you've made the conscious decision to leave on time on Tuesday and strike the dynamic bargain with yourself, almost magically the small stuff drops off. You focus on bigger, more crucial tasks or responsibilities. On the first Tuesday, and certainly by the second or third, you begin to benefit from *a system of self-reinforcement*, whereby the rewards you enjoy (leaving the office on time, actually having an evening free of work-related thoughts) are so enticing that you structure your workday so as to achieve your reward.

Eventually, when you add Thursdays, then Mondays, then Wednesdays to the process, you begin to reclaim your entire workweek. A marvelous cycle is initiated. You actually

➤ Leave the workplace with more zest.

➤ Have more energy to pursue your non-work life.

➤ Sleep better.

➤ Arrive at work more rested.

➤ Are more productive.

As you increase the probability of leaving another workday on time, you perpetuate the cycle and its benefits.

Leaving on Time Whenever You Want To

How does it all start? Declare that the following Tuesday will be an eight- or nine-hour workday and nothing more. You leave on time that day feeling good about what you've accomplished. That's it—no grandiose plan, no long-term commitment, no radical change, and hardly any pain.

Go!
Silently repeat to yourself "I choose to easily leave at closing time today and feel good about it." Never mind if at first you think this mantra doesn't have any power. Do it. You'll find yourself leaving more often, more easily, and on time.

Recall how long you've been in your profession, and that you are in your present position for a lengthy run. On no particular day and at no particular hour are you rooted to your desk. You're a professional. You got the job done previously; you'll get it done now as well. Feel free to go.

If, during a given day you've decided you're going to leave on time, it becomes obvious you have more to do than you can get done that day (and when won't that happen?), etch out exactly what you're going to *begin on* the next morning. This will reduce any anxiety or guilt you feel about leaving on time. Ultimately, you'll have no anxiety or guilt. After all, you have a life, don't you?

Let everyone in your office know that you're leaving at five or whatever closing time is for you. Announce to people, "I've got to be outta here at five today," or whatever it takes. *People tend to support another's goal when that goal has been announced.* Some people may resent you for leaving on time; fortunately, some others may not. You must decide whether to let other people's reactions control your actions.

If you insist on a list of "steps," here's what you can do on that first Tuesday, or any other day, to leave on time when you choose to:

1. Announce to everyone that you have a personal commitment at 5:30 that evening. If you have a child, you could say your child is in need of important parental assistance. Schedule something for 5:30 that evening if it helps.

2. Mark on your calendar that you'll be leaving at five.

3. Get a good night's rest the night before.

4. Eat a light lunch; it keeps you from being sluggish in the afternoon.

5. Strike a dynamic bargain with yourself at the start of the day, in late morning, in early afternoon, and in late afternoon. (Remember, it's okay to modify the bargain to accommodate a changing situation.)

6. Regard any intrusion or upset as merely part of the workday.

7. After striking the dynamic bargain with yourself, don't be tempted to add more items to your list at the last minute.

8. Envision how you'll feel when you leave right at closing time (even so, there is no reason for you to be staring at the clock for the last 45 minutes).

9. Late in the afternoon, ask a coworker to walk you out at closing time.

This list is long; ensuring that you leave the workplace on time may seem too involved to accomplish. If you engage in *only two or three of these steps*, however, you'll still get the reinforcement you need.

What a Concept!

This chapter is intentionally simple, if for no other reason than this: The more you have to do and have to remember, the less you'll do and the less you'll remember. Your only assignment: *Leave work on time.*

The Least You Need to Know

➤ You deserve to leave on time—*at least* occasionally—and to feel good about it.

➤ Depending on your organization's culture, you may have to use one or more of the strategies discussed in this chapter to leave on time.

➤ The changes you need to make have to be easy to put in place and easy to follow. If they're too difficult, they won't hold. Winning back your time requires only small steps, but a progression of them.

➤ To leave on time, start with one day per week (such as Tuesday) and get to the point where you can leave on time every Tuesday for an entire month.

➤ You can strike a dynamic bargain with yourself to feel good about what you've done, choose what else you want to accomplish, and feel good about leaving.

➤ As you develop the habit of leaving on time, you develop a positive cycle of being even more productive while leaving on time more often.

Chapter 2

Who Knows Where the Time Goes? (Actually, You'll Know)

In This Chapter

➤ A cheerful subject: how much longer you're likely to have on the planet

➤ The activity that sucks the time out of your life

➤ The cumulative impact of devoting small segments of time daily to things you don't enjoy doing

➤ Why simplifying things is important now, and will become ultra-important in the future

Have you ever stopped to consider how much time you have in your whole life, and how much time you've spent on various activities? Suppose you graduated from college at the age of 22, and in the course of your life expect to work about 48 years, bringing you to age 70. Over the course of those 48 years, how much time would you suppose you spend on routine activities such as working, sleeping, watching television, other recreational activities, eating, and commuting?

Here's the typical breakdown, based on various demographic studies and my own calculations:

Working	16 years
Sleeping	15 years
Watching TV	5 to 7 years
Other recreation	2 to 4 years
Eating	3 years
Commuting	2 years

It's amazing when you look at the cumulative total of the time you'll spend engaged in these activities during your productive work life, isn't it? Suppose that you're already 30-something and on average will live another 45 years. Thus, you have about 30 *waking* years left, and about 20 years to accomplish whatever you're seeking to accomplish. That realization alone may help you focus your time. If it doesn't, maybe you're asleep right now.

If you're thinking, "Hey, I'm 35 now, but I don't expect to reach age 80," think again. The Society of Actuaries estimates that if you're female and you're 40 years old, your life expectancy is age 85 (see Table 2.1). For males it's slightly less, age 80.3.

Table 2.1 Life Expectancy of Americans

FEMALE		MALE	
AGE NOW (Years)	**EXPECTED LIFE (Years)**	**AGE NOW (Years)**	**EXPECTED (Years)**
40	85.0	40	80.3
50	85.5	50	81.1
60	86.3	60	82.6
70	87.9	70	85.0

Data from the National Center for Health Statistics shows that every 25 years since 1900, the life expectancy of both men and women has increased by about five to seven years. The increase in life expectancy for people born between 1975 and the year 2000 may be as much as nine or ten years (see Table 2.2).

Table 2.2   Life Expectancy of Americans (from Birth, by 25-Year Intervals)

FEMALE		MALE	
YEAR BORN	EXPECTED LIFE (Years)	YEAR BORN	EXPECTED LIFE (Years)
1900	48.3	1900	46.3
1925	57.6	1925	55.6
1950	71.1	1950	65.6
1975	76.5	1975	68.7
2000	85?	2000	79?

On average, you're likely to live longer than you think you will. If you think you're going to reach 75, you may well reach 85. If you think you'll reach 85, you may hit 95!

The realization that you may live much longer than you think necessitates developing some longer-term perspectives about how you want to spend your life. (I'll cover these in greater detail in the last few chapters of the book.)

Limits Help You Be Productive

With decades to go, it's easy to get caught in the trap of delaying the activities and events you promised yourself you'd undertake. Whether life seems short and merry or long and boring, there's only so much of it. Architect Frank Lloyd Wright once observed that people build "most nobly when limitations are at their greatest." You can use the limits on your time or resources to achieve your most desired accomplishments.

Consider how productive you are, for example, right before you leave for a vacation, or how well you do on a task when a deadline's been imposed (even though you might not enjoy *having* the deadline, or like the person who imposed it). As one who's written several books in the last couple of years, I can testify about deadlines. Each time I signed a book contract, I had to deliver a specified number of manuscript pages in coherent order, and accomplish what I said I would do by a certain date. These contracts with their deadlines *imposed limits* that helped me be productive.

Warning
Whether you have 30 or 60 years left, it will be to no avail if your days race by, you wake up thinking *I'm already behind*, you stay late at work night after night, or let stuff pile up and then feel exhausted because you can't get to it.

These limits may not always appear helpful or supportive, yet you undoubtedly have many of them confronting you. Here are some examples of limits you may be facing right now:

➤ You have to pick your kids up by 5:30 each weekday.

➤ You have to turn in a work log on Fridays.

➤ The author of this book said you need to leave the office most days by 5:00 p.m.

➤ You can work about nine hours daily before your mind turns to mush.

➤ Your hard disk is almost full and you have no intention of spending more money for disk space.

➤ Your contract is ending in eleven weeks.

➤ You have only 24 minutes left on your lunch break.

➤ The Post Office closes at 5:00 p.m. every evening.

➤ The oil in your car needs changing after another 300 miles.

➤ A loved one has only about three or four months to live.

➤ You get paid every two weeks.

What limits do you face in your career or personal life that you could actually employ to propel yourself to higher productivity? Once you learn to harness these for the benefit they provide, you begin to reclaim your time. I suggest that your daily, number one limit be *finishing your day so that you leave work at the normal closing hour.*

What Steals Your Time?

After examining the problem for many, many years, combing through extensive research, interviewing dozens (even hundreds) of people, collecting articles, tapping the insights of many learned people, I found that the number one element that robs people of their time can be boiled down to a single word. (Please be sure you're in a chair that can support your full weight in case you slump over when the answer is revealed to you.)

Okay, if you're ready, take a deep breath, because here's the revelation of the ages. The number one activity on this planet, in this country, in your life, that steals your time (here it is—I hope you're ready for this): television.

Is there anything I can say in a couple of pages that will help you to cut down on the amount of TV you watch? Consider the findings of TV-Free America, a public service organization in Washington, D.C. that has compiled some rather startling data about television viewership in America.

The average American watches more than four hours of TV each day, equal to two months of non-stop TV watching per year, and equal to more than 12 solid years of non-stop TV watching in the life of a person who lives to age 72. (I know you're not average...of course you watch less...)

➤ 66% of Americans regularly watch TV while eating dinner.

➤ 49% of Americans say they watch too much television.

➤ 19% of Americans say they would like to read or visit friends, but have no time!

What a Concept!

About 90 million adults watch television for at least two hours on any Monday and Tuesday night, equal to 360,000,000 viewer-hours. The 1 billion viewer-hours used up in one month, if applied elsewhere, could transform the nation. If (like many Americans) you watch *four* hours of TV on those two weeknights, those vanished eight hours could make a significant difference in your life.

Ah, but you're an adult and you can choose to watch TV whenever you want, can't you? Or can you? Increasingly, I find that television is a drug, similar to drugs you might ingest. As the Internet predictably becomes a dominating aspect of more people's lives, eventually it will replace TV and be even more seductive. Information, news, and entertainment are starting to merge. Do you feel yourself being sucked into the vortex of infotainment?

Not So Amusing

In his book, *Amusing Ourselves to Death*, Dr. Neil Postman says that entertainment is the dominant force of public discourse in society, affecting the arts, sciences, politics, religion, and education. Certainly entertainment has a necessary function in your life: It stimulates thinking. It can be liberating to your soul. It can give you a break from the drudgery or monotony of daily living. Of note, entertainment can free you to explore new ways of thinking, new ideas, and new possibilities.

The harm in being over-entertained—which everyone now faces—is that your life seems to pale by comparison. What is the true cost of entertainment? Certainly your time, and usually your money. You're willing to trade these because entertainment expressly is not reality. It's designed to be "superior" to reality—at least more titillating and more engaging. Fantasy sells almost as much stuff on TV as sports, and a lot more stuff than reality would. In a 1978 lecture at Indiana University, the late Gene Roddenberry summed it up this way: "TV does not exist to entertain you. TV exists to sell you things."

When compared to what you see on the screen, your own life may seem dull and plastic. Instead, it is real and holds great potential. Ultimately, the quality of your life and the memories of your life will depend on what you actively did, not what you passively ingested (such as seeing *Forest Gump* for the third time). What will you do in the next month to enrich your life—*actually* enrich it? *Who* will you meet? *Where* will you go? *What* will you risk?

Consider how much time and energy you're willing to spend with your favorite TV personalities. Now contrast this with how much time you actually spend with any of your neighbors.

Neighbors. You know—those near-strangers next door. Do you even care about their lives? They are, in fact, flesh-and-blood people, with real strengths, real weaknesses, and real lives. They may even have the capacity to be your lifelong friends. Do they offer as much pleasure to you, however, as the fantasy heroes on *Star Trek*, Kevin Costner in his latest role, or Claudia Schiffer simply posing in garments you'll never own? You might have a reason to like your neighbors: Consider all the expensive stuff they're *not* trying to sell you.

But I Only Watch the News—Just to Stay Informed

I know people who habitually watch the nightly news under the guise of being an informed citizen. The problem is, most of what passes for news on television—isn't. It's merely a replay of what television news tends to give you over and over.

I'm sorry (who isn't?) that there's drug infestation in America and that teenagers get pregnant, or that there are homeless people roaming many cities. Unless you're going to take *action* on any of this stuff, however, watching another report about it doesn't really count as news to you. A better term for all of this would be "the sames." For television coverage of these phenomena to be news, there would have to be something *new*. A continual replay of society's ills doesn't represent news, it represents "the sames."

Tonight, if you choose to watch Dan Rather or Peter Jennings, consider how much of what you're seeing is the same as last week, last month, last year, or even 10 years ago. Hey, maybe they ought to rename it something like "The ABC Nightly Sames with Peter Jennings."

Look, I'm not saying you shouldn't watch any news. I'm saying you should understand the context in which news is presented. News shows are designed to attract viewers so sponsors can sell things, the same as any other show; they heighten the emphasis on some stories and completely ignore others. As long as you understand the limitations of TV news, watch away! Just don't turn off your brain when the news comes on.

Children and Television

Maybe you didn't watch as much television as kids today are watching, but you probably watched a lot, and the habit is ingrained. Kids today, however, are going to set some all-time records. Here's what TV-Free America found about children's television viewing:

➤ The number of minutes per week that parents spend in meaningful conversation with their children is 38.5.

➤ The number of minutes per week that the average child watches television is 1680.

➤ 50% of children aged 6 to 17 have television sets in their bedrooms.

➤ 70% of day-care centers use TV sets during a typical day.

➤ 73% of parents would like to limit their children's TV viewing (but apparently they don't or they can't).

As if you're not watching enough television, what are the chances that you're turning on the radio, cluttering up your mind as well? I know, I know, if you listen to the radio on the way to work, how can that possibly be stealing your time? Well, it is. Consider a friend of mine who liked to listen to a West Coast shock-jock in the morning. Year after year, my friend Bill was titillated on his way to work by the shock-talk.

In essence, he settled for an electronic fix, another type of drug if you will, that briefly took him out of his own life and into some form of contemptuous humor that got him through the next 10 minutes (or however long) on his way to work. After all the years of listening, my friend is not empowered, energized, or any better able to face his day. Obviously, however, he isn't alone; this particular shock-jock has become a multi-million-dollar media franchise with strong ratings for more than a decade.

Warning
Most American children, notes Dr. James Twitchell, author of *The Carnival Culture*, begin watching television before they can talk. A child at age 6 will have invested more hours watching television *than in speaking with his or her father over an entire lifetime.*

So sad.

Warning
Don't make the erroneous assumption that watching brain-drain TV or listening to shock-talkers on the radio has no impact on your time. They vacuum up time you could have used.

If you listen closely to the shock-jocks of the world, you can sometimes detect that they are angry people. They vent their anger through a form of broadcast that has (for whatever reason) become a socially tolerated route to riches.

Question: How many shock-jocks does it take to change a light bulb?

Answer: Three—one to throw the bulb away, one to stick his finger in the socket, and one to yell about it on the air.

What Could We Do with the Time?

Instead of listening to the radio on his drive to work, Bill could contemplate what he'd like to achieve for that day. If he has meetings, he could consider some of the points he would like to make. He might visualize having a pleasant lunch with a coworker. He might put on some classical music to ease his mind as he makes his way through the otherwise-unforgiving rush-hour traffic.

If he consciously chooses to play the radio, perhaps he can listen to classical music (which has been demonstrated to have a soothing impact on listeners). Maybe he'll switch to a provocative newsmagazine-type show where important issues are covered with some depth and perspective. Perhaps he'll tune into something else that truly stimulates his intellect.

Of course, he has the option of playing CDs or cassettes. He can listen to famous speeches, motivational programs, or entire books on cassette. He can play cassettes of famous radio programs of yesteryear or listen to the Bible on cassette. By applying a modicum of creativity, he can turn his commuting time into something special. He can turn his use of the television into something special.

My friend has many different pockets of time available. He also has many options— *choices he can make*—to determine how he spends them.

So do *you*.

Jeff Davidson's 10 Steps to Kick Electronic Addiction

Okay, I can hear you railing, "I'm not giving up television. There are some worthwhile things on TV, and I *can* turn it off whenever I want." If that's so, then fine—but if you're hooked and you can't admit it to me, perhaps you can admit it to yourself. Here are 10 techniques you can use to get yourself "unplugged":

➤ Go a whole weekend without turning on a radio or television.

➤ Call your friends (both local and out-of-town) one evening per week instead of watching any television.

➤ Return to hobbies such as stamp collecting, playing a musical instrument, gardening, or playing word games one other weeknight, instead of watching TV.

➤ Allow yourself to *selectively* watch two hours of programming each Saturday and Sunday for one month.

➤ Permit yourself one high-quality video per weekend during another month. The video has to inspire, inform, reflect history, be biographical, or be otherwise socially redeeming. Stop watching "shoot-em-ups," chase scenes, and films that titillate but add little to your life.

➤ If you walk or jog with a Walkman, undertake these exercises three times in a row without such a device, so you can experience another way to jog: naturally taking in what you pass on your trip.

➤ Recognize that rightly or wrongly, you've been programmed since birth to tune in to electronic media for news, information, entertainment, and diversion. It's by no means your only option.

➤ Look for others seeking to wean themselves from electronics. Is there a book discussion group? How about a bowling league, outing club, or biking group?

➤ *Attend* sporting events rather than viewing the same type of event on television. Watching a good high school baseball team or women's collegiate tennis match can be as rewarding as watching major-league baseball or Wimbledon, respectively. And you visibly support the athletes by being there.

➤ Recognize that the number of videos, CDs, computer games, and other electronic items competing for your attention exceeds the time you have in life to pay homage to them.

A Simple Formula for Reclaiming Your Time

While the cumulative impact of being hooked to electronic media is considerable, the cumulative impact of doing what you don't like to do—like household tasks—is equally insidious.

Recall the example of your 48-year career—graduating college at age 22 and working until age 70. Here's a quick way to see that you need to delegate or cast off those things you don't like to do. Any activity in which you engage for only 30 minutes a day in the course of your 48-year productive work life will take one solid year of your life! Any activity in which you engage for only 60 minutes a day will take two solid years of your 48 years. How can this be so?

Think of it as a math course most of us never had in school: Numbers That Really Mean Something. One-half hour is to 24 hours as one hour is to 48 hours. That's true by the good old commutative principle of arithmetic. Likewise, one hour is to 48 hours as one year is to 48 years.

For you math buffs, here it is in equation form:

> 1/2 hour is to 24 hours as 1 hour is to 48 hours,
> or .5/24 =1/48

> 1 hour is to 48 hours as 1 year is to 48 years,
> or 1/48=1/48

Go!
Identify those activities you currently handle yourself that could be handled some other way.

When you take off one-forty-eighth of your day (only 30 minutes out of 24 hours) the cumulative effect over 48 years is to take one year of your 48 years. There's no way around it. If you clean your house, on average, for 30 minutes a day, in the course of 48 years you've spent the equivalent of one solid year, nonstop, cleaning your house.

This immediately tells you that if you can't stand cleaning your house (or engaging in anything else you don't like) for an average of 30 minutes a day, *stop doing it*. I don't mean let your house get filthy; hire somebody to clean your house, clean it yourself less often, or find some other alternative. Why? Because the time in your life is being taken up; the cumulative impact of doing what you don't like to do, as just illustrated, is that your precious years are being consumed—time you simply cannot reclaim under any scenario.

"Well, that's fine to pay somebody to clean the house, but ultimately I'll be paying people for all kinds of things I don't like to do, just so I can have more time." Yes! Exactly. In Chapter 6 I'll get into this in spades.

What can you list as those things that you know you need to stop doing because they are taking up valuable time in your life? For openers, here are some suggestions:

➤ Cleaning the house.

➤ Reading the newspaper (or is it the *samepaper*?) every day. If it makes you late for work or prevents you from handling higher-priority activities, only do it now and then.

➤ Cutting the grass, or any other yard work. (See Chapter 7 about when it makes sense to pay others to do it.)

➤ Fixing your car.

➤ Cooking.

➤ Reading junk mail because it's addressed to you. (Don't laugh. I know many people who feel *compelled* to read their junk mail. "Hey, somebody took the time to send me this.")

➤ Reading every godforsaken e-mail message zapped over to you.

➤ Answering the phone.

Let's Not Confuse Issues

If you enjoy engaging in some of these activities, keep doing them. Perhaps you can do them a little less; perhaps there's another way to proceed. Your goal is to delegate or eliminate those tasks or activities which you can't stand doing. Kevin Trudeau, a memory expert, says, "Don't manage something if you can eliminate it altogether." Not bad advice.

When my contact-lens routine was becoming a bore—taking them off, cleaning them, lubricating them, and so forth—I was able to save several minutes per day by switching to a new type of contact lens that's thinner, requires little maintenance, can be worn 16 or 18 hours a day with no irritation, and after several days, can simply be chucked.

What have you been putting off that you could handle right now, knowing you would simplify your life? I wouldn't be offended if you stopped reading a moment, closed the book right now, and gave this question the full consideration it merits in your life—unless, of course, *Melrose Place* is coming on.

The Least You Need to Know

➤ You're probably going to live longer than you think, but it will be to no avail if your days continue to race by full of frustration and the same old stuff.

➤ To the extent you can reduce your television viewing, you'll experience an abundance of more time in your life.

➤ The cumulative impact of doing what you don't like to do is profound. 30-minute, 20-minute, even 10-minute savings per day are significant, and will dramatically affect the amount of discretionary time you have in your life.

➤ If drudgery sticks you up for either your life's time or your money, which would you rather hand over?

➤ Don't manage what you can eliminate altogether. Simplify what you can't eliminate.

Chapter 3

Living Longer but Enjoying It Less

In This Chapter

➤ Why the time-pressure you face is not a personal shortcoming! ("Hey, I already knew that!")

➤ The time-pressure problems that others report they are experiencing ("You too?")

➤ Five converging factors that conspire to consume your time ("Gotcha!")

➤ The future: more choices competing for your time and attention than you ever imagined ("Where's it all going?")

You are now armed with two major principles. From Chapter 1, you learned that the key to winning back your time is to redevelop the habit of getting your work done within the course of a normal eight- or nine-hour workday. In Chapter 2 you saw that even small segments of time each day have a dramatic impact on the amount of time in your life over which you *have* control. The dilemma of an entire culture, however, is that everyone is feeling time-pressed—and feeling as if he or she is a poor time manager, and as if somehow he or she is at fault. (Know the feeling?)

It may *not* be your fault, and you're not alone. The problem you face is a wide-sweeping phenomenon more than a personal one. Fortunately, there are various measures you can take in your career and life to win back more of your time, and that's what this book will examine.

Let's see how to live longer and enjoy it more.

Everyone's in Virtually the Same Boat

Suppose that all of society *was* in a hurry (which at most times seems exactly correct). People would have to do more all the time, in *less* time. Sound familiar? The evidence is mounting that time has become the most valuable commodity in society. A study titled "Time Pressure in the '90s," conducted by Hilton Time Value Surveys, found that folks feel just plain rushed:

Warning
Simply being born into this culture at this time all but guarantees that much of your day will be consumed if you're not careful.

➤ 77% of people surveyed selected "spending time with family and friends" as their top goal in the '90s.

➤ 66% said they would put more emphasis on "having free time."

➤ 38% report cutting back on sleep to *make more time*.

➤ 33% said they are unlikely to be able to make time for their ideal weekend.

➤ 33% said they don't accomplish what they set out to do each day.

➤ 31% worry that they don't spend enough time with their families and friends.

➤ 29% constantly feel under stress.

➤ 21% said they don't have time for fun anymore.

➤ 20% reported calling in sick to work at least once in the past year when they simply needed time to relax.

Why Such Feelings of Time Pressure?

In my earlier book, *Breathing Space: Living and Working at a Comfortable Pace in a Sped-Up Society*, I identified five mega-realities that have an unconditional impact on everybody all the time. The factors include:

➤ An expanding volume of knowledge.

➤ Mass-media growth and electronic addiction.

➤ The paper-trail culture.

➤ An overabundance of choices.

➤ Population growth.

Does it seem as if these factors are ganging up on you? If so, it's time to divide and conquer—examine them one by one and suggest some strategies.

Knowledge

Knowledge is power, but how many people feel powerful? Many Americans fear they are underinformed. The volume of new knowledge broadcast and published in every field is enormous; it exceeds anyone's ability to keep pace. All told, more words are published or broadcast *in a day* than you could comfortably ingest in the rest of your life. By far, America leads the world in the sheer volume of information generated and disseminated.

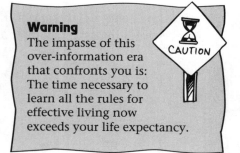

Warning
The impasse of this over-information era that confronts you is: The time necessary to learn all the rules for effective living now exceeds your life expectancy.

This is why so many books designed to help readers be more effective in managing their time fall wide of the mark. They list dozens, if not hundreds, of rules—and you already have more "rules for being effective" to follow in your career and life than you can comfortably keep track of. I doubt that *feels* very effective.

What a Concept!

The key to winning back your time is to be more effective at *being* rather than *doing*.

If this sounds like mumbo-jumbo, let me say it another way: To win back your time ultimately means *having less to do*, not more. Doing the "less" I'm talking about means carefully identifying what's vitally important to you, which is the subject of Chapter 6.

Media Growth

As you'll remember from Chapter 2 (and probably from personal experience), the effect of the mass media on people's lives continues unchecked. In America, more than four out of

Go!
If you feel better about your own life, it's easier to empathize and take action on behalf of those who need help. For one thing, you have a little more time to do so.

five households own VCRs. In 1972, three major television networks dominated television—ABC, NBC, and CBS. Soon there will be 500 full-power independent television stations. Many cable TV subscribers receive up to 140 channels that offer more than 72,000 shows per month. (Bruce Springsteen understated it best: "Fifty-seven channels and nothin' on." It may soon be 5,700. Same complaint.)

With its sensationalized trivia, the mass media overglut obscures fundamental issues that *do* merit concern, such as preserving the environment or feeding the starving.

Paper Trails

It's like being a computer overloaded with data, or a detective swamped with too many eyewitness reports. Having too much paper to deal with makes you feel overwhelmed and overworked. Americans today are consuming at least three times as much paper as 10 years ago. There are two basic reasons why American society spews so much paper:

Word Power
In *Future Shock* (1970), Alvin Toffler used the term **overchoice** to describe the stress that comes from too many options, especially the so-what variety. In paperback the book itself was a classic example: you could buy it with a blue, orange, or hot-pink cover.

➤ We have the nearly lowest postal rates in the world.

➤ We have the most equipment that can generate paper.

The typical executive receives more than 225 pieces of *unsolicited* mail each month, or about 12 pieces daily. Annually the average family receives more than 200 catalogs they did not request—on top of those they *did* request.

An Overabundance of Choices

Having choices is a blessing of a free market economy. Like too much of everything else, however, having too many choices leads to the feeling of being overwhelmed. Currently more than 1,260 varieties of shampoo are on the market. More than 2,000 skin care products are currently selling. Some 75 different types of exercise shoes are now available, each with scores of variations in style, functions, and features. Every choice demands time; increased time expenditure means mounting exhaustion.

Population

Not only are you not alone, you're less alone all the time. From the beginning of creation to 1850 A.D., world population grew to one billion. It grew to two billion by 1930, three billion by 1960, four billion by 1979, and five billion by 1987, and six billion is en route. Every 33 months, 257,000,000 people (the current population of America) are added to the planet.

Each *day*, world population (births minus deaths) increases by *more than 275,000 people*. Geometric growth in human population permeates and dominates every aspect of the planet, its resources, the environment, and all living things.

One could argue that having all these new people around makes the world more hectic, its people more competitive for fewer economic niches, and employers more apt to see the labor force as a cheap commodity whose personal time they can claim willy-nilly. To accept the increasing effects of population pressure is to accept the reality of current human existence. I don't see how you can ignore it.

Population Growth Alone Robs You of Time

The effect of rapid increases in population alone has a dramatic impact on the pace of society and your life. Predictably, more densely packed urban areas have resulted in a gridlock of the nation's transportation systems.

It *is* taking you longer to drive merely a few blocks; it's not the day of the week or the season, and it's not going to subside soon. Our population and road use grow faster than government's ability to repair highways, bridges, and vital urban arteries. In fact, vehicles (primarily cars) are multiplying twice as fast as people, currently approaching 400,000,000 vehicles, compared to 165,000,000 registered motorists.

The roads aren't going to clear up soon—it would cost more than two trillion dollars over the next 30 years to repair and maintain the nation's pipes, tunnels, cables, and roads. 39% of the nation's bridges are in need of major repairs. Do you cross a bridge in the morning? Do you experience frequent delays? More than half of the heavily traveled roads in America that link urban and suburban areas are in fair to poor condition. Is it any wonder you dissipate a good chunk of your time getting to work—and home from work—each day?

Some 86% of American commuters still get to work by automobile, and 84% of inner-city travel is by automobile. The average American now drudgingly commutes 157,600 miles to work during his working life, equal to six times around the earth. Commuting snarls are increasing. City planners report there will be no clear solution to gridlock for decades, and population studies reveal that the nation's metropolitan areas will become home *to an even greater percentage of the population.*

Crowding makes urban space harder to traverse, which eats up more time; hence the less space there is, the less time there is. Even suburban areas will face unending traffic dilemmas. If only the gridlock were confined to commuter arteries. Not so. Shoppers, air travelers, vacationers, even campers—everyone in motion—is (or will be) feeling its effects. We'll get to counteracting them in a minute; for now, consider some of these "locks" on your time:

Airlock

If you haven't noticed, airline passenger traffic nearly tripled since 1980. Concurrently, there are fewer nonstop flights, particularly on cross-continental trips. Airport expansion trails the increased passenger loads. Worse, all airlines pad their scheduled departure and arrival times—extended more than 50% since 1980—to appear as if they're not late, while actual air time remains about the same. When you're scheduled to board at 10:10 a.m., that is simply when you're supposed to be seated in the plane. Rollout from the gate is always later. Consequently they're as slow and late as ever, but now they're within the promised limits.

If you're not already doing it, bring plenty of work (or another diversion) with you so you can remain productive (or at least calm) despite flight delays.

Camplock

On an average summer day, Yellowstone Park has more visitors than the population of Houston. Other national parks across the country are faced with swarms of visitors; campsites are in high demand. While the federal government is making good progress to restore the parks, in the meantime vacationers have to contend with traffic lines to get into the parks, lines for concessions, and waiting lists for campsites.

Hereafter it may make sense to do your camping Tuesday through Thursday—whenever the masses are not—or find "undiscovered" parks closer to home.

Shoplock

If all 258 million Americans went shopping at the same time, each would have 18 square feet of retail space. There is more retail space in America today than ever before. Despite the dramatic increase in catalog and TV shopping, shopping malls still always appear crowded. Waiting for a parking space can take 10 minutes, unless you are willing to park in the far reaches of some lots. Once inside, you have to jostle through crowds to get to shops, movie theaters, and restaurants—and that's on slow days. During the holidays, you get the worst.

Maybe it's time to shop-by-catalog with more fervor.

Cyberlock

With the increasing number of people going online—combined with the inability of major online services to meet the increased demand—cyberlock is in full swing. Several-minute waits to be connected are common (to a computer, even one minute is an eon). Cyberlock could easily become a long-term phenomenon as even more people go online for longer periods of time, sending and downloading ever-larger volumes of information.

Are you willing to log on at 3:00 a.m.? It would help (as long as you don't make a habit of disrupting your sleep).

> **Word Power**
> What gridlock, airlock, camplock, shoplock, and cyberlock tell you is that it pays to be a **contrarian**—a word I like that means "somebody too stubbornly individual to do what everybody else is trying to do at once."

Avoiding Lines, or Time-Shifting 101

If you find yourself perpetually waiting in lines, try time-shifting to avoid crowds. No, you don't need a time machine—just your good sense. For example:

➤ Go get your movie tickets early, take a walk, and then return three minutes before the picture starts (after everyone has already filed into the theater). There are always available seats, even for twosomes; theater management knows exactly how many tickets they're selling for each showing. You might not get the front row, but who needs the neck strain anyway?

➤ A different approach to movies: Go to the theater early for the first showing, buy your tickets, go in and take a seat, and for the next 20 minutes or so listen to your favorite music with a Walkman headset.

➤ If you commute, rather than going earlier or later, explore not going in at all—telecommuting. (I'll discuss this in detail in Chapter 5.)

> **Go!**
> To avoid the locks that so many others encounter, commute at different times, fly at different times, camp at different times, shop at different times, and get online at other times than the masses.

➤ To avoid airlock, fly in the day before and fly out after everyone else has. Schedule vacation travel time, particularly Thanksgiving and Christmas, as much as six months in advance. You might stay home during those times and travel when everyone else isn't, namely the week after the holidays.

➤ To avoid camplock, patronize some of the less-traveled national and state parks. There are more than 200 national parks and thousands of state parks; most do not experience hordes of visitors.

➤ To avoid cyberlock, consider getting online later (say, after ten) if you're on the West Coast; most East Coast users will have gone to bed. If you're on the East Coast, get online early (say, 6:00 or 7:00 a.m.); most West Coast users will still be asleep.

➤ To avoid shoplock, make more purchases by catalog—but be careful of how and when you give your name out. Otherwise you'll be inundated by dozens of other catalog vendors. You probably have a fax machine at work, and you may even have one at home. Shopping by fax has never been easier. It's actually a great time-saver because your name, address, phone, and fax number are accurately submitted to vendors, along with your order, order number, and the price.

Saving Shopping Time

"Shop till you drop" is often too true for too many. Why do it? The list in this section contains a host of tips you can use to budget your time more effectively and feel less stressed when shopping (in general, and when holiday shopping in particular):

➤ Spend a few minutes at home or work contemplating what you are going to buy and for whom. Then draw up a list and bring it with you—this will help keep you focused and less prone to becoming overwhelmed once you're inside the stores.

➤ Instead of being buffeted by the crowds at the large shopping malls, shop at stores in small commercial strips or with free-standing locations.

➤ Consider ordering by mail if there is still a while to go before the holidays—but ask that your name be kept off the vendors' direct-mail lists. Receiving dozens of unwanted catalogs throughout the year diminishes your *breathing space* and contributes to landfills.

➤ Reduce the strain of carrying large bundles by choosing smaller-sized gifts such as jewelry, compact discs, cassettes, gloves, sunglasses, and so forth.

➤ Shop on Monday, Tuesday, or Wednesday evenings. Avoid weekend shopping!

➤ Give yourself frequent breaks while shopping. It is not a marathon event. There is absolutely no reason to make shopping for friends and loved ones anything but a joyful experience. Lighten up!

➤ If you find a gift that would please many of those on your gift list, such as chocolates or a book, buy multiple quantities in one transaction to reduce overall shopping time.

➤ When buying holiday gifts and cards, make your shopping count three and four times. Think of who is having a wedding, birthday, or baby soon. It may mean doing a little more shopping now, but you'll avoid many more trips in throes of January, February, and March.

➤ Once you get the packages home, take them to your table, desk or wherever you're going to *complete the shopping trip*—you still have to remove tags and stickers, file the invoices, wrap items, mail some of them, and store others.

➤ Designate one evening for greeting cards—if you send out cards, send them all out the same evening; then they're out of the way and en route.

What a Concept!

From now on, you're likely to experience other forms of "lock" in whatever career or personal endeavors you undertake. Engaging in activities at times when the masses are not has never been a more useful option. Become a contrarian!

The simple reality of today and of your life (not to mention everyone else's) is that society will grow more complex every day for the rest of your life. (Wow—what an existence.) Who gets the blame? As we'll see in the next chapter, nobody.

The Least You Need to Know

➤ Simply being born into this society, at this time, all but guarantees that increasingly you will feel pressed for time.

➤ The time pressure you feel is largely not your fault.

➤ More choices mean more time spent choosing.

➤ Shop, travel, camp, and drive when others are not. Time-shift away from crowds whenever you can.

➤ Use store services when shopping such as catalog ordering, delivery, and gift-wrapping.

Chapter 4

It's Not Your Fault (and It's Not Mine, Either)

> **In This Chapter**
>
> ➤ Social complexity happens!
>
> ➤ The basics for approaching a new task, learning a new procedure, or assimilating new information
>
> ➤ The virtue and wisdom of slowing down
>
> ➤ How your checkbook and your time are inextricably linked
>
> ➤ Abdicating low-level choices

As a professional speaker, I often address groups at annual conventions and conferences. I am no longer amazed at the ever-growing variety of professional associations that have not only been established, but actually have thousands of members. For example, there is (whether you believe it or not) a National Association of Sewer Service Companies, a Cranial Academy, a Medieval Academy of America, a Society of Certified Kitchen and Bathroom Designers, a Society of Wine Educators, and even an International Concatenated (the spelling *is* correct) Order of Hoo-Hoo. Ho-ho.

More people, more groups, more information generated, where's it all leading? One result is that the amount of information that competes for your time on a daily basis is on the

Etched in Stone
No one can keep up.

rise—and taking a staggering toll. You may have an M.B.A. degree, you may have ten years of management experience under your belt, and you may have read every book on time management in creation. Nevertheless, you can't keep up. You are not alone—and you are probably not to blame.

Self-Esteem Is Not the Issue

If you feel any diminished sense of self-worth or self-esteem, ease up. This is a characteristic response when human beings are overexposed to stimuli.

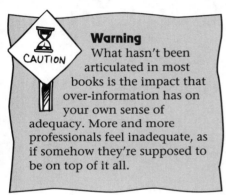

Warning
What hasn't been articulated in most books is the impact that over-information has on your own sense of adequacy. More and more professionals feel inadequate, as if somehow they're supposed to be on top of it all.

Feeling time-pressed today is not connected to how you were raised, it's not a question of where you went to school, where you live, your profession, or who you married. Even individuals who display high self-worth and high self-esteem often have too many concerns competing for their time and attention; they feel extreme time pressure. Even people who set goals—and do it well—frequently feel overwhelmed.

If you can accept the notion that the dissipation of your career and personal time is probably not your fault, you're already well on the road to winning back your time.

Like Drinking from a Rain Barrel

Suppose you were extremely parched and the only way you could quench your thirst was to lift a rain barrel and try to eke out a few sips at a time. This feat would require impressive strength and balance, but why waste it on such a difficult way to drink? If you take a small cup, stick it in the rain barrel, and extract a couple of ounces at a time, you could easily quench your thirst. Now consider the daily information deluge. When you attempt to take in everything that's flung your way, the predictable response is that you drown in information (and still don't quench your thirst).

Tackling new information—such as navigating the Internet, integrating another technology into your work routine, or assimilating other changes—is smoother when you employ *basics*.

What are basics?

1. Follow directions.

2. Take one step at a time.

3. Assess where you are every couple of steps.

4. Having determined that you are on the right path, continue.

Information comes to you at a breakneck pace, and that pace will accelerate day after day for the rest of your life. Don't bite off more than you can chew; sometimes *simply slowing down* is the best response to "too much of too much" competing for your time and attention. Slow down so that you can figure out the best way to proceed.

Go!
At all times, your goal is to scoop out information in amounts you can digest, and tackle activities in amounts you can do.

The Virtue of Slowing Down

When I speak to audiences about these dilemmas and discuss potential solutions, I ask, "Do you want it fast, or do you want it to last?" Hereafter, I'd like you to begin practicing a new response when a lot is thrown at you: *momentarily pause.*

I saw a clever book title that sums up the philosophy here: *Don't Just Do Something, Sit There.* Too often, the reflex to take action only exacerbates your time-pressure problems. I'll tackle this head-on in Part 4.

What a Concept!

Give up trying to stay on top of it all, which only ensures that you'll fall farther behind. Nobody today can keep on top of everything, nor is the attempt worthwhile. What you *can* do—and this is quite a lot—is make choices about where (and to what) you'll direct your time and attention.

Your Checkbook and Your Time

Has there ever been a nation in the history of the earth that accumulated huge deficits over a prolonged period of time, lacked a concerted effort towards reducing these deficits, and was able to sustain economic prosperity for its citizens?

No, this isn't a paid political announcement. What I'm basically asking you is: Can a nation (or a person—*you* in particular) run up huge deficits and expect no consequences? Chances are you have some financial deficits. (Lucky guess, huh?) For decades, millions of

Americans have accumulated personal debt via credit cards, loans, and other forms of financing. Such sustained deficit spending eventually erodes your ability to prepare for the future, and worse, to capitalize on current opportunities.

What's all this got to do with winning back your time? Well, it's an exercise in fiendishly simple math: The more you owe, the more enslaved you are! Dr. Judith Schor, in *Consumerism*, says that chances are you've been taught to consume way past your needs. As time passes, I find (and you may have hit upon a similar insight) that the more material possessions I own, the less I feel in control of my time. During my college days and early twenties, when I had little, I felt the freest.

Right now, how would it feel if all your credit cards were paid off? How would it feel if you paid your monthly rent or mortgage several months in advance? How would it feel if your car loan was paid off? How would it feel if you were actually able to pay some of your utility bills for months in advance? For most people it would feel wonderful. You'd feel in control of your time. I know, because I do this; more to the point, the time you spend worrying would be reduced to zip.

I know the arguments about losing the interest I could have earned on the money if I pay for the electric bill three months in advance. Ah, but wait. A month after I've paid my electric bill three months in advance, I get the next month's bill. Guess what? It shows that I have a huge credit and that *nothing* is due. I *smile* when I see bills like these. So will you. This approach frees you twice: Not only is the bill already paid (which robs the bill of its wet-blanket effect), but you've freed yourself from having to fight the reluctance to *sit down and pay it now.*

A Moratorium on Spending

To reduce your personal financial deficits, I suggest placing a moratorium on spending, regardless of what items entice you, until your credit cards have zero balances. Now, please, let's not confuse issues. In Chapter 2, I discussed briefly a theme I'll return to, in detail, in Chapter 7: the value of paying others to do that which you don't like to do. These are separate issues: Impulsive spending is not the same as investing in your freedom.

What a Concept!

Paying for something that frees up your time is a life benefit. Paying for material things that you don't need (and certainly don't save your time) may be satisfying, but ultimately can be draining.

Here are some useful exercises for controlling your checkbook and winning back more of your time:

1. **Write out checks to pay bills in advance of their due dates**. Then, keep an advance file with a folder for each day of the month. Place the check in a sealed, addressed, stamped envelope. Then put the envelope in the folder of the day it's to be mailed. This way the money is allocated in advance in your checkbook, and your bills are paid on time. If your checking account pays interest (for you "interest" buffs) it also means that you don't lose interest.

2. **Once in a while, overpay the balance due on your continuing accounts or pay early.** This will give you the aforementioned psychological boost when you see a credit on your next statement, and give you a good reputation with your creditors—which could come in handy in the future.

3. **Keep a stick-on note in your checkbook for an immediate reference that lists what's coming in this month and what needs to go out.** This provides you with a running mini-cash-flow list that you can refer to any time. Update it every couple of weeks, or days, if necessary.

4. **Look back through your old checks and carefully see what you paid to whom for what.** Do the same thing with your monthly credit card statements. Put a red mark next to all those expenditures that you didn't need to undertake, or that in retrospect you could have done without.

5. **Now, considering expenditures on the horizon, which ones can you do without?**

As author Roger Dawson says, it doesn't matter how much money you're making; if you're spending more than you take in each month, you're headed for trouble.

A Mind-Boggling Array of Choices

Another fundamental reason you might not be enjoying the time of your life as much as you did a year (or five years) ago is the number of choices you continually confront (one of the "mega-realities"). While flying from Denver to San Francisco and flipping through one of the airline magazines, I came upon an ad for jelly beans. You remember jelly beans, Ronald Reagan's favorite snack? When people in my age group were growing up, how many different colors of jelly beans where there? Six, maybe eight? Let's see green, black, pink, red, yellow, blue, and orange?

The ad I saw had names and pictures—if you can believe this—of 48 types of jelly beans. Banana mint swirl. Peppermint polka-dot patty. Lazy lime sublime. What's a kid to do?

(I have tasted some of that company's product, including jalapeño. Weird, but fun. Of course, if you're going to habituate kids to overchoice, you've gotta start 'em early....)

Actually you've got it no better. Go into an athletic shoe store today and the clerk asks you, "What'll it be, air up, air out, pump up, pump down?" Go into a bike store and the clerk asks you, "10-speed, 15-speed, 21-speed, men's, women's, mountain bike, trail bike, or racing bike?" The same phenomenon occurs when you go to buy a tennis racquet, an exercise machine, a whirlpool bath, or even a birdbath—no kidding, you have to shop for a birdbath to appreciate the overabundance of choices that can suddenly confront you. (Mmm. I wonder if it matters to the birds. Maybe someone has already surveyed them or, better yet, perhaps Uncle Sam has commissioned a $565,000 study to gain a fuller grasp of the situation while sliding further into inextricable national debt...no, I am not a candidate...at least not yet....)

The *New York Times* ran a major feature saying that people are experiencing stress and anxiety today when shopping for (excuse me?) *leisure goods*. There are so many choices! Weighing such choices takes up your time. The problem is worse in the workplace.

An Explosion of Choices at Work

Consider all the vendor product catalogs you're retaining. How about all the flyers for management training seminars? How about magazine and newsletter subscription offers at incredible savings? How about the coffee service options that await? Everywhere you turn, you see, you're confronted with more choices than you can comfortably respond to.

Careful, You're Using Up Your Life on These Choices

Every moment adds up. If you spend a lot of them contemplating which product or service to choose from among dozens or hundreds, you are consuming considerable amounts of your time. Even when you choose, however wisely, it isn't once and for all. Next week, next month, next year a new, better, faster, sleeker, less expensive, more powerful version of your product or service will be available. It will be that way for the rest of your life. (And these choices are only some of the small stuff. In Chapter 14, I'll discuss making *big* decisions in record time.)

Your unrelenting responsibility to *keep choosing* is another relatively unarticulated aspect of being born into this culture at this time. Its cumulative effect is the robbing of your time.

> **Warning**
> At first blush, it wouldn't seem as if a plethora of choices is such a bad thing. After all, what can be the harm in having a wide variety of options available? The answer is that there is great harm in filling precious time with nagging-but-trivial decisions.

As often as possible, avoid making such low-level choices. If the same yardstick is available in red, blue, yellow, or white and it is all the same to you, grab the one that is closest or take the one that the clerk hands to you.

Whenever you catch yourself making a low-level decision, consider: does this make a difference? Get in the habit of making only a few decisions a day—the ones that count. For the low-level stuff, reclaim your right to say, "Who cares?"

Who Decides How You Spend Your Time? You Do!

Many people proceed through their day and their lives as if others were in control of their time. Do you fall into this category? Right now, look at the upcoming list and put a check mark next to any party list you believe is "in control of" your time.

❏ Your parents?

❏ Children?

❏ Community?

❏ Company president?

❏ Coworkers?

❏ Your industry?

❏ Government?

❏ Governor, mayor?

❏ Television, radio?

❏ Spouse?

❏ Neighbors?

❏ Landlord or mortgagor?

❏ Boss?

❏ Peers?

❏ Opinion leaders?

❏ U.S. President?

❏ The press?

❏ Unknown forces?

When I ask people in seminars to complete this checklist, most catch on quickly and leave all the boxes unchecked. The one box that does get checked, if any, is Boss. There *are* bad bosses, unreasonable bosses, workaholic bosses, and even psychotic bosses. I've had them all! (See the section on "Managing Your Boss" in Chapter 9.) Your boss may pile on the assignments, but you're the one who determines how, largely when, and often with whom you'll tackle them.

The degree to which you believe that your boss or anyone else controls your time, however, is the degree to which you'll have to struggle to win back your time. Denis Waitely, author of *The Psychology of Winning*, says that you are in the control booth of your life (unless, of course, you relinquished control and then forgot you ever *were* in control).

Becoming a Consultant to Yourself

Perhaps you have no problem acknowledging intellectually that you are, in fact, in control of your time. In practice, you may find this a bit more difficult. An article I once read taught me a technique for proceeding when confronted with too much stuff competing for my time and attention. It originated with none other than Richard Milhous ("I am not a crook") Nixon, America's thirty-eighth president. Nixon practiced the notion of *becoming a consultant to himself.*

When you're faced with many choices (what decision to make, which road to take, which dish to bake), pretend that you are a highly-paid consultant—to yourself. If your last name is Smith, your internal dialogue would begin as follows: "What does Smith need to do next?" You proceed as if you are able to separate from your physical shell, moving to a corner of the room and observing yourself from the vantage point of an objective third party.

By referring to yourself in the third person ("What does Smith need to do next?"), you derive different answers from those you'd get if you simply thought, "What should I do next?"

How so? Well, there's a semantic shift that happens when you refer to yourself as if you were an observer. Apparently this practice opens a channel of discovery not readily available to you otherwise. (Maybe it has to do with whether you're seeing the forest or the trees....)

When can you use this technique? When *can't* you use it? Becoming a consultant to yourself works as well in crunch times as it does in milder times. A variation on this theme is to pretend a real-life trusted advisor or mentor is there with you. Ask yourself how he or she would advise you.

To Thine Own Self Thou Mayest Turn

Whether it's becoming a contrarian, taking one step at a time, spending less and keeping your debts to zero, being more prudent about the information you ingest, remembering who's in control, avoiding low-level choices when possible, or becoming a consultant to yourself, you can always turn to *yourself* for the important task of safeguarding your time.

What a Concept!

You are more resourceful than you often acknowledge, and you always have more options than you know.

The Least You Need to Know

➤ Social complexity will continue and will make you feel less in control, and it has that effect on everybody; your ability to manage your affairs is not a self-worth or self-esteem issue.

➤ The health of your cash flow directly influences the control you have over your time. Spend more, work longer, watch your control disappear.

➤ Every day for the rest of your life you'll face a mind-boggling array of choices competing for your time and attention; you can use up valuable time in your life on the less important choices. Avoid low-level decision-making if possible.

➤ Take one step at a time. Don't be afraid to slow down temporarily.

➤ You get to decide where you spend the time in your life, not your boss, not your landlord, not your spouse, not the press, not the mayor, not the president. Become a consultant to yourself whenever you need to have third-party objectivity.

Chapter 5

Get Real About What You Want

In This Chapter

➤ The importance of choosing and supporting only a handful of priorities, not two dozen

➤ The accumulation of health, wealth, or wisdom is a gradual process

➤ How to reinforce your priorities and support your goals

Deciding what is important to you is a key to winning back your time. If you don't decide what's important to you, almost anything can compete for your time and attention—and thereby dissipate your day, your week, your year, your career, and your life! Once you decide what's important to you, you can then become a consultant to yourself to determine what it actually takes to maintain or achieve what you've designated as important. (If it seems the pieces are starting to fit together, read on. If not, read on anyway; they will.)

"There is no inherent problem in our desire to escalate our goals, as long as we enjoy the struggle along the way."

Mihaly Csikszentmihalyi, *Flow: The Psychology of Optimal Experience*

Getting real about what you want means being honest with yourself. It also means taking the time and trouble to compose a list of priorities and reviewing your list often until your priorities sink in. (I know you've encountered this type of advice before, but if you had followed it well, you probably wouldn't have bought this book! Call it a hunch.)

What a Concept!

If you don't know where you're going, any road will take you there.

Okay, So What's Important to You?

The great paradox about priorities is that if you have too many of them, then by definition they can't *all* be priorities. Do you have 15 or 18 things that you list as top priorities in your life? If so, you'd better look again, because no one has time to pay homage to 15 to 18 "top" priorities. Life doesn't work that way.

To help you identify what your priorities are, let's look at the concerns that traditionally have served as top priorities for many people. I'm not saying that your list has to match this one—it probably won't—but this is a starting point:

➤ Family

➤ Society

➤ Health and well-being

➤ Wealth

➤ Career growth

➤ Intellectual growth

➤ Spiritual growth

Let's tackle each of these (suggested) priority areas one by one with some concrete examples. Keep in mind that you may have others, not listed here, that are appropriate for you.

Family—the Folks on Your Side

For most people this is Numero Uno. If you're married and you love your spouse, being with your spouse is easily a top priority. If you have children and you love them, same situation. If you're single, your priority may be to find a spouse and to raise a family someday, or to treat the people closest to you like a "chosen family." If you're in school, it may be to spend time with your nuclear family, your mom and dad, your brothers and sisters.

If family is a top priority, then one of your goals may be to listen to your spouse in earnest for at least 35 minutes three times per week. (Won't he or she be pleased as punch if you listen at all, never mind *three* times a week!)

Likewise, there are a variety of other goals you can choose to support your priority. Here is a quick list of other possible goals related to family:

Go!
As with all the priorities to be discussed, you want to attach goals—specific, action-oriented steps with timelines—to your priorities to reinforce them. Write them down too.

➤ Take the children for a day-trip once every two weeks.

➤ Have an annual photo of the family taken every other December; as a shared family project every year, put some old photos in a family chronicle.

➤ Have or adopt one or more children within seven years. (There are a lot of kids already out there who need good homes.)

➤ Send flowers to your spouse, unannounced, once a month.

➤ Buy life insurance to ensure your family's prosperity in the event of your demise. (Maybe you'd better not announce this one, either.)

➤ Begin an annuity so you can more easily afford your child's college education by the time he or she is ready to enter college 12 (or however many) years hence.

Many of the goals that support your family priority are related to other priorities such as wealth, intellectual growth, and so forth. (That's understandable; it's wonderfully efficient when you set goals that address more than one priority.)

Society (Social Priorities)

If you want to do something about society's woes (*besides* yell at your TV set), it means participating in your community—helping it be the best it can be. It could mean being involved with religious, social, fraternal, or community groups. You might choose to run for local office—not for purposes of ego gratification, but to give something of value back to the community. Here are some possible goals that may support your social priorities:

➤ Volunteer to serve on the Welcome Wagon Committee for new residents this fall.

➤ Contribute to the XYZ campaign in the forthcoming election.

➤ Begin an environmental-awareness movement in your town by the first day of spring.

➤ Recycle your paper, plastic, glass, and other recyclable materials every week hereafter.

➤ Run for town council for the next term.

➤ Write, by the end of this summer, an article on the importance of nurturing America's youth.

➤ Be the host to a foreign exchange student during the next academic year.

➤ Chair this season's March of Dimes campaign in your region, or volunteer on a Habitat for Humanity project.

➤ Send one e-mail message per month to the major networks concerning the major violence on television.

➤ Coach a community-league sports team.

➤ Volunteer every two weeks at a local homeless shelter or kitchen.

➤ Tutor a student from your local elementary or high school.

➤ Participate in a community theater or choral production.

Jumpin' Jehoshaphat! You may quickly surmise that it takes time and energy to support your priorities. But wait a minute. If your goal is to win back your time, why would you want suggestions for *new* stuff that you're not currently undertaking? The answer: Tasks in support of your priorities do indeed help you win back your time. It's less of a mystery than it might seem.

What a Concept

The few things that you'll do in support of your priorities will take far less time than all the things you do now in support of God-knows-what.

When you have 15 to 18 priorities, you're involved in many tasks, some personally rewarding, some not. *There is an inherent efficiency in identifying your priorities and establishing some goals to support those priorities.* Any other way of proceeding in life is analogous to jumping on your horse and riding off in all directions. (You *can* put a stick of dynamite under your saddle, but why?)

Health and Well-Being

It's true. Even I (your author!) have been duped. After a decade and a half of staying in top shape, surrounding myself with others who were doing the same, and reading articles that reinforced my beliefs about fitness, I thought all of society was also focused on health and well-being. Then I came across a report in the *Journal of the American Medical Association* that says the number of overweight Americans gained steadily in the past decade.

One-third of people over age 20 tip the scales in the wrong direction. On average, adults weigh eight pounds more than they did a decade ago, says Dr. Robert Kuczmarski and colleagues at the National Center for Health Statistics, Hyattsville, Maryland. "Comparisons…indicate dramatic increases in the prevalence" of overweight people, Kuczmarski said. No less than 33% of adult Americans are overweight today, compared to 25% in 1976, according to Carlos Crespo of the National Heart, Lung, and Blood Institute. That figures out to about 58 million.

Dr. F. Xavier Pi-Sunyer of St. Lukes-Roosevelt Hospital Center, New York City, observes that "while our caloric intake increases, our caloric expenditure decreases." He also takes a dim view of duff-sitting: "Sedentariness has become a way of life." (Slow and short, but a way of life.)

Couch potatoes, beware! This area is—you guessed it— another gold mine of worthy places to put time and energy. There are dozens of possible goals you could have in support of your health and well-being priority. Here's a quick list; though not all may be for everyone, consider them in the light of your situation and lifestyle:

➤ To join a health club within a month and set a goal of working out four times per week for at least 30 minutes.

➤ To buy five healthy foods you've never tried.

➤ To take two health-and-fitness books out of the library, read them cover to cover, and gain at least five new ideas you'll put into practice within one month.

➤ To become a lifetime member of a local bicycle club, walking club, or exercise group.

➤ To begin going on walking and hiking dates rather than going to restaurants and movies.

➤ To hire a fitness trainer in February.

➤ To get a good night's sleep at least five times per week (more on sleep in Chapter 8).

➤ To have an annual check-up every January (especially important if you live alone and don't cook).

➤ To take daily the vitamin supplements that meet your needs, as determined by a dietitian.

➤ To imbibe 50% less alcohol per week, starting this week.

➤ To make one weekend hike of at least six miles every weekend.

➤ To visit a nutritionist or dietitian this month to determine your nutritional needs.

Go!
Check with your doctor before you start any exercise or diet program, of course—especially if you haven't been exerting yourself much. You'll get two benefits: (1) valuable (maybe life-saving) guidance and (2) a kick out of the look on the doctor's face.

The great thing about having well-being as a priority is that it gives you a license to engage in all kinds of social and personal behaviors that you might not have otherwise. Picking up a piece of litter in a neighbor's yard, for example, is good for you, is good for the neighbor, and is good for the community. I know a man who carefully tucks a five-dollar bill into the last 50 pages of classic novels on the shelves at the local library. He wants to anonymously reward people, albeit in a small way, who read such books. If you're thinking, "Yeah right, five bucks down the drain…," perhaps you're simply not ready for this level of well-being.

Wealth

I'm guessing that accumulating outrageous wealth isn't one of your priorities, so I won't spend too much time on this one…. Just kidding. Far be it from me to say that accumulating wealth is evil. The Bible says the *love of money is the root of all evil*. It doesn't say that money *per se* is the root of all evil. You can accumulate as much wealth as you want, as long as you don't love your money more than you love people, or love your country.

There are all kinds of wealth: intellectual wealth, spiritual wealth, and so forth. These are about to be covered in subsequent pages, so let's confine the focus to economic wealth. Here are examples of goals you could choose in support of this priority:

➤ I will call a certified financial planner this month and pay him or her to advise me about how to invest for the future.

➤ I will start an IRA by this Friday and contribute x amount of dollars each month until I reach the maximum contribution level.

➤ This week, I will redirect my employer to automatically invest x amount from my paycheck in a 401(k), mutual fund account, or other investment.

➤ By next quarter, I will lower the number of deductions on my paycheck so I get a larger refund from the IRS after filing taxes at the end of this year.

➤ I will join an investment club this month, meet with the members regularly, learn about investment opportunities, and participate in intelligently selected group investments.

➤ During my next performance review, I will ask for a raise and offer irrefutable supporting evidence that spells out the merits of my request.

➤ (For sales professionals) I will earn $\$x$ in commissions for the fourth quarter of 199X.

➤ By September 30, 199X, I will launch the business venture of my dreams.

➤ By the end of this month, using the spreadsheet on my computer to calculate cash flow, I will trim monthly expenditures by $400.

➤ Within six months, I will live within my means.

➤ I will open a retirement account with my credit union next week.

➤ I will bring my lunch to work at least three times per week.

➤ I will choose an automobile that gets better gas mileage.

The not-so-funny thing about amassing wealth is that for most people it's a long-term affair. Only a tiny, tiny fraction of the population ever wins the lottery. (If you've ever thought you stand a better chance of getting struck by lightning, you're probably right.)

What a Concept!

Wealth, like happiness and fitness, is a habit. You get wealthy by developing habits of wealth.

You add to your net worth a little at a time. Gradually, inexorably, the wealth begins to build. *Fortune* and *Forbes* articles on wealthy Americans reveal that the majority got wealthy slowly. Many wealthy folks developed a habit, early on, of living within their means, and awoke one fine day to find that their nest egg had grown to a sizable sum. Wow, what a country! *What a way to win back your time, by developing habits of wealth, breaking the cycle of deficit spending, and eventually accumulating a sum that enables you to do what you want in life!*

Career Growth

Beyond what's already been discussed, the pursuit of career growth per se may be one of your priorities. If you've invested years in getting to be where you are, and like what you do, you may naturally look forward to rising within your industry or profession.

Independent of the monetary rewards, there's a high level of inner satisfaction among those who are highly learned and well respected in their chosen fields. Among the many kinds of goals you can choose in support of your career-growth priority, try these on for size:

➤ To read one new book a month by the top authors writing in your field.

➤ To subscribe to (or start reading in your company library) two important industry publications you don't currently receive.

➤ To form a monthly study group (with four to eight colleagues you respect) so that you each encourage each other in learning more about your chosen fields.

➤ To register to attend a conference this week (or submit a proposal to make a presentation of your own there).

➤ To return to school to get a graduate degree in your field.

➤ To undertake original research over the next six months, put your findings in an article, and pursue getting it published in a prominent industry journal.

➤ To complete the certification process in your industry by December 31, 199X.

➤ To volunteer for that special task force forming in April.

➤ To join your professional association or (if you're already a member) run for office in it.

As society grows more complex (and by now you know it will), it may behoove you to become more of a specialist in your chosen field. Perhaps you could focus on biology, more specifically marine biology, then marine biology restricted to a certain class of species, then marine biology in certain species restricted to Hudson Bay. If you're among a handful of specialists in your niche, then wealth tends to follow.

One caveat: It only pays to specialize *if* you know your specialty is marketable and has long-term prospects (as some of my friends know from bitter academic experience).

What a Concept!

The more specialized you become, the more potentially valuable you become to those who need your expertise.

If you're worried that becoming too specialized will restrict your intellectual diversity, fear not. What generally happens is that once you decide on pursuing a highly narrow field and concentration, it actually expands. You begin to see things within your narrow focus that you couldn't have seen before making the choice.

Intellectual Growth

When Supreme Court Justice Oliver Wendell Holmes was in his eighties he was asked why he was reading a voluminous book, *Plutarch's Lives*. He responded, "To improve my mind." Rumor has it that the pursuit of intellectual growth—*independent of career growth*—is a worthy priority. Certainly education and intellectual development—for its own sake, and for that of your children—rank at the top of any list of priorities you may devise. In support of this priority, here's a smorgasbord of possible goals:

➤ To read one new book every two weeks that is not in my field and not connected to what I do for a living.

➤ To spend time with my children playing games such as Scrabble to help develop their vocabulary and love of words.

➤ To enroll in that local community college course I've been wanting to take.

➤ To send away for a books-on-tape catalog, so I can listen to the classics rather than having to read them (since I already read way more than I want to).

➤ To take at least one international trip per year to a destination completely foreign to me so I can learn firsthand about other cultures.

➤ To sign up for the lecture series sponsored by the local Chamber of Commerce so I can hear firsthand from visiting authorities on contemporary issues.

➤ To drop my subscription to, say, *People* magazine (sorry, *People*!) and replace it with (for example) a subscription to *Smithsonian* magazine.

➤ To watch at least one program per week on The Learning Channel or PBS.

➤ Rent a documentary rather than a feature film.

➤ Read an historical account instead of a mystery.

As more people go online via the Microsoft Network, CompuServe, America Online, Prodigy, and other online vendors, it will become progressively easier to enhance intellectual growth. (Wait a minute. People used to say that about television in the '40s, didn't they? Uh-oh...) It's worth an early warning: Watch out. You can get hooked on the Internet far worse than you can get hooked on television. You can be sitting at your monitor at 7:00 p.m., look up, and notice it's 12:30 in the morning. Those commercials about "Where do you want to go today?" belie the insidious nature of the Net.

> ## What a Concept!
>
> As with life priorities, you need some priorities before sitting down and simply freewheeling on the Net. Otherwise, rather than winning back your time, you'll watch it dissipate among an infinite number of *seemingly* intellectual pursuits.

Next time someone tells you to "get real," consider this reality you've already got: There are far more worthy and stimulating issues competing for your time and attention *than you will ever be able to come close to pursuing.* It takes strength to stay within the confines of a few pre-identified focus areas, while of course *occasionally* allowing yourself to freewheel all over creation. (You are, after all, only human, aren't you? Know the feeling.)

Spirituality

This is a vital subject that's ticklish to handle. I've known lots of folks who are extremely sensitive about religion, even to the point of taking offense where none was intended. So let me pause to point out that (1) I'm not assuming that your spiritual tradition is the same as mine or (2) prescribing my own practices. Spirituality is a wellspring of the quality in life. The time that makes up an enjoyed and appreciated life is well worth winning back.

Spiritual growth doesn't necessarily mean going to church every Sunday, although it certainly can involve that. Your spiritual growth can occur anywhere at any time. If you choose to seek active spiritual growth as a priority, goals like these can support your choice:

➤ Taking at least one walk per week in a natural setting and appreciating your surroundings.

➤ Deciding to actually *read* the holy book for your religion during the next 12 months or listen to it on cassette.

➤ Beginning to live as if you recognize that every creature on earth is a divine creation. You can start this anytime, and the ending time is never.

➤ Practicing the art of forgiveness by making three calls this week to people against whom you've held long-term grudges, and telling each of them that you forgive them. ("Do I *have* to do this?" Yes, if you're serious about your well-being.)

➤ Giving thanks each morning or evening for all you have been given in life.

➤ Deciding to regularly attend weekly religious services.

➤ Donating your time and energy once a month to a food service for the homeless, starting in May.

➤ Scouring your home this week to find everything you can donate to the less fortunate.

➤ Listening to inspirational music.

➤ Praying for yourself and for others.

Okay, enough of the "be as good as you can be" stuff! You already know a lot of possible starting points.

That's seven possible priority areas we've looked at so far—and even they are not the be-all and end-all. You may have some that don't fit within these categories at all. That's fine, as long as you recognize what they are and choose goals that involve specific action steps and timelines in support of your priorities.

A Blueprint for Getting Started

To support the priorities you choose, here are some basic action steps:

➤ Write down everything that's important to you or that you want to accomplish in your life. A long list is okay.

➤ Several days later, reexamine the list. Cross out anything that no longer strikes your fancy. Feel free to add a few things if they come up.

➤ In another day or so, look at your list again and see whether any items can be grouped together. Then reword or relabel those choices. At all times, feel free to drop an item if you think it's iffy.

➤ Put your list away for yet another day. (I know this is going to take a week or more!) Then review it again.

➤ Once more combine, regroup, or delete things on the list as it appears appropriate to you.

➤ Prepare the final draft of your list, recognizing that in time it may change. For now, these are what you've identified as your priorities.

Got Your List? Shrink It

Maybe what this country *really* needs is a good portable priority list. At any rate, *you* can have one. If you have several fonts in your printer, print out your list in a reduced point size (or simply hand-print it in miniature) so it's small enough to carry in your wallet or purse. Then review your list of priorities at least once a day. With so many other things competing for your time and attention, it's easy to lose sight of your priorities by ten in the morning. It's not excessive to read your priority list several times a day (unless, of course, they're all in the same half hour).

What a Concept!

Some of the most accomplished people who appear to be in great control of their time "know what they're doing" for a reason. Quite simply, they review their priority lists all the time.

The Least You Need to Know

➤ Deciding what's important to you is a key to winning back your time efficiently. Once you've identified your priorities, you're likelier to make progress toward them—and more often—each day.

➤ The great paradox about priorities is that if you have too many of them, then *by definition* they can't all be priorities.

➤ Traditionally, the top priorities for many people have been family, society, health, and well-being, wealth, career growth, intellectual growth, and spiritual growth.

➤ To establish your priorities, write down everything that's important to you, reexamine the list, cross out anything that no longer strikes your fancy, add a few things if they come up, group similar items, reword or relabel any of your choices, and prepare the final draft of your priority list.

➤ Print your list in a reduced point size so it's small enough to carry in your wallet or purse; review it often.

Chapter 6

What Will It Really Take to Support Your Priorities?

In This Chapter

➤ Making sure you support your priorities with goals you'll follow through on

➤ The telltale signs that you're heading off course

➤ The effect commuting has on your time and whether telecommuting may be for you

➤ A neat way to manage your to-do list and balance short-term and long-term tasks

Big decisions are *not* "once and for all"—unless they have a lot of everyday decisions to keep them company and make them stick.

Suppose you identify your priorities and establish some goals in support of them. What will it actually take to ensure that you stay on your chosen path? It's easy to stray—*you* know it and *I* know it.

Here are some reinforcement techniques you can put to use:

1. Join others who have priorities and goals similar to yours—and are supporting them. Perhaps there is a professional, civic, or social organization in your town that fills the bill.

2. Surround yourself with reinforcing statements, reminders, and self-stick notes so you don't lose sight of what you said was important.

3. Create a cassette tape of your priorities and supporting goals in the form of affirmations, "I choose to visit the health club four times per week for a minimum workout of 30 minutes...."

4. Prepare a budget to help determine exactly what it will cost to honor your priorities and the goals you've chosen to support them.

5. Develop rituals that support your quest. For example, if your goal is to lose six pounds by the end of June, begin taking the stairs instead of the elevator whenever you're heading down for lunch or to your car at the end of the day.

6. Keep your action steps bite-size. There's no value in choosing goals that are so difficult to achieve that you're not honoring the associated priority at all.

7. Report to someone. Have some significant other serving as a coach or watchdog to ensure that you do what you said you were going to do. (Don't be lulled into thinking that this ploy is only for the weak-willed. High achievers do this!)

8. Visualize the goal every day, while you're waiting in a bank line, when you're in the bathroom, when you're stuck in traffic. Olympic athletes aboard a plane, en route to their next meet, can actually improve their performance during the meet when they visualize their performance during the plane ride.

9. Set up a series of small rewards so that you're naturally reinforcing the behavior in which you've chosen to engage.

10. Contract with yourself. Freelance writer Dennis Hensley describes *advancement by contract*: "A contract takes precedence over everything else. For example, you make your monthly house payment rather than use the money for a vacation because you have to make that payment: the contract allows the bank to repossess your home if you do not fulfill your obligation."

    He suggests carefully selecting three to five major goals (in support of your priorities) and then signing a contract that aids you in reaching them. "Once under contract, you would have to succeed by a selected date or else face the consequences of defaulting on the contract." (It's worth remembering that in the business world, people who default can be sued or go unpaid for the work done to date.) Make three copies of your contract (this chapter includes an example). Keep the original. Give one copy each to your spouse, a trusted coworker, and a friend.

SELF-INITIATED CONTRACT

I, _____ , agree to accomplish each of the following items on or before
_____ and hereby do formally contract myself to these purposes.

These goals are challenging, but reasonable, and I accept them willingly.

A. _____

B. _____

C._____

Signature: _____ Date: _____

Review your contract when you find yourself becoming distracted by small details or if you think you are not moving in the right direction.

11. Plot your campaign on the calendar. Start from the ending date (the deadline for completing your goal) and work back to the present, plotting the subtasks and activities you'll need to undertake.

Proceeding in reverse through the monthly calendar helps you establish realistic *interim dates* that reflect not only your available resources, *but also* vacations, holidays, weekends, other off-duty hours, and *reasonable output levels*. A sample Calendar Block Back in this chapter follows.

CALENDAR BLOCK BACK

MONTH _____MARCH_____ YEAR _____

SUNDAY	MONDAY	TUESDAY	WEDNESDAY	THURSDAY	FRIDAY	SATURDAY
	1 Submitted Feb. 24	2 Deliver draft workshop planning report	3	4	5	6
7	8	9 Submitted to typing	10	11	12	13
14	15 Assessment of conf. capabilities Deliver profile revisions	16	17	18	19 Assessment of target audience, 52 pages Deliver	20
21	22	23	24	25	26	27
28	29	30	31 Deliver final workshop planning report			

Start with a major deadline, then work backward to set realistic interim dates for achieving what you want.

61

What a Concept!

Give yourself flexibility; build in some downtime, vacation time, and so forth. Devise a realistic plan to accomplish your goal by the time you said you would.

When You Get Off Course

If you're like most people, then on more than one occasion (I'm being kind here) you're bound to get off course. When you do, revisit the list just given and initiate a new strategy in place of—or, better yet, in addition to—the ones you're using. Here are some warning signs that you're not following the path you said you would:

> ➤ *You've talked a good fight, and that's all.* You said this undertaking was important to you—but you haven't scheduled any time on your calendar, budgeted any funds, or even thought about it.

Go!
If you're serious about winning back your time, you'll consider moving closer to work. If that's not an option, strongly consider telecommuting.

> ➤ *You're late.* You said that working out four times a week was important; by the third week, you're making excuses to yourself about why you're *not*.

> ➤ *You've let piles of paper stack up.* Although you've chosen only a handful of priorities, you find yourself still wading through stuff that's nice, interesting, *and not that important.*

> ➤ *Your goals missed the mark.* Despite the toil, time, and thought you put into establishing your goals, it's apparent they're not supporting your priorities.

Is Commuting Depleting Your Time?

As you consider what it will take to pursue the goals that support your priorities, sometimes creative solutions begin to appear. For example, imagine reducing the aggravation and wasted time of a fundamental act discussed in Chapter 2: simply getting to your workplace. For many people, it's a pretty horrendous undertaking.

So let's talk about telecommuting.

Reach Out and Touch Your Screen

As metro areas keep expanding, and daily commuting becomes more trying, telecommuting is becoming popular. At least 20 million people are doing some telecommuting these days, at least periodically. Telecommuters complete much of their work back in the traditional office.

The benefits to you include reduced commuting time; reduced personal cost for travel, clothing, and food; flexible working hours; more time for dependents; and potentially greater autonomy.

You can rack up significant time savings by telecommuting, as detailed in Table 6.1.

Word Power
Telecommuting is working outside the office (that is, away from your employer's base of operations) and staying in touch with co-workers via electronics—computer, fax, and phone. It can be done from your home, a hotel, a satellite office, or even your car.

Table 6.1 How Commuting Adds Up to Lost Time

Round-Trip Minutes/Day	Hours/Year	Equivalent Number of 40-Hour Weeks
40	160	4
60	240	6
80	320	8
100	400	10

Believe it or not, the federal government is on your side when it comes to telecommuting! In 1990, the Clean Air Act mandated that all businesses employing more than 100 people in a single location reduce their employees' commute time by 25 percent. Employers could encourage the use of public transportation, car-pooling, condensed work weeks, *or telecommuting*. The act is now being implemented, primarily in the states with the worst pollution.

Maybe you can sell your employer on this trend. The benefits to them include potentially higher productivity; reduced office or plant costs; the ability to accommodate physically challenged employees; and the ability to motivate new employees with an attractive stay-at-home-and-get-paid option.

Stockbrokers, consultants, writers, and even top-level executives are finding that telecommuting enables them to maintain—even increase—their overall productivity.

Jobs such as computer programming, translating, software engineering, sales, and system analysis are well suited for telecommuting. Other professions such as word processing, book publishing, telemarketing, research, and architecture also lend themselves to effective telecommuting.

So far, telecommuting has been employed only marginally. Some employees have been directed to telecommute; others have requested the option. In business and government, however, the vast majority of employees do not telecommute, even periodically.

Even on a limited basis, telecommuting can provide you with many benefits beyond the time saved by not commuting. These include cost-savings, as well as the freedom to focus on projects, initiate conceptual thinking, and exercise more control over your environment. Check it out!

Managing Your To-Do List, Long-Term Versus Short-Term

Whether you telecommute or work in a traditional office five days a week—whether you've identified your priorities (and some well-chosen goals to support them), or are still stuck in old habits—it's likely you face an age-old dilemma: staying on top of all the things you need or want to get done.

People are always asking me about *to-do lists*. Do they need to maintain them? How can they go about fixing them? Everyone I know in the workaday world uses *some* kind of list as a tool for getting things done. I'm neither for nor opposed to any particular system you might use to stay efficient; judge by results. (Chapter 12 will explore some time-management tools and technologies.) If you maintain some type of to-do list, you can use it to support your priorities—by *lengthening* it for strategic reasons, *without* overloading yourself. Read on.

The "Superlong" Strategy

The primary dilemma you're most likely to face is balancing short-term against long-term tasks and activities. Believe it or not, I maintain a 12- to 14-page to-do list! I have hundreds of things on my to-do list, *arranged by major life priorities*. How do I keep from going crazy? Most of what's on the list are *medium- to long-range activities*.

The first page of my list represents only the short-term activities—those I've chosen to do now or this week. I draw continually from the 14-page list, moving items to the top as it becomes desirable (or necessary) to tackle them.

In essence, I maintain a *dynamic to-do list*; it contains everything on this earth I want to get done, but always there's *only one* page I need to look at: the top page. Yes, I am forever updating the list and printing out new versions, but there are so many advantages that I wouldn't think of doing it any other way.

My list is long, and it will stay long. I don't worry about all the things on the list because I know I can get only so much done in a day, a week, and so forth. I also know I'll review the entire list periodically, always moving items from say, page 8, up to the front page. Thus my anxiety stays at a rather low level.

Not Everything Every Day

Many days, I don't look at pages 2 through 14. Also, keeping the list on my computer is handy; virtually all word-processing programs contain word-search capabilities. If I'm working on something during the day and it appears there will be a breakthrough in my ability to tackle something *else* that's buried on page 8 or 9, I have only to search for a word or phrase, and I quickly come to the item. There is no need to dig through the hundreds of items on the list.

Maintaining such a long to-do list also helps me become more proficient in managing long-term or repeated tasks. If I'm working on a long-term project, I can continually draw from it those portions that can be handled in the short-term; I move them up to the front page. Likewise, if a task is a repeat or cyclical project I have to do every month or every year, I can choose a portion to get done and move into the short term (up to the front page).

Go!
If you have not considered using the superlong to-do strategy, give it a try. Chances are good your first superlong list will fill two to five pages—it should be easy to move items up to the front as needed. You'll have a clear idea of what you face—all on one big roster—and keep your priorities sharp for years to come.

Short-Circuiting the To-Do List

On occasion, you can short-circuit the to-do list and get stuff done without even entering it on your list. Here's how it works. Most people who encounter information worth retaining make a note or add it to a list; it may stay there for days or months. To deal with it faster, remember that useful information usually involves calling or writing to someone else. Rather than adding it to your to-do list try a fast-action option:

➤ Pick up a pocket dictator and fire off a letter or memo.

➤ Type a message on your computer for immediate transmission by fax, e-mail, or Internet message.

I was talking to someone who enjoyed the *Readers' Digest* section in which Peter Rich reviews vocabulary words from books he's read. Years ago, I would have made a note about this (and dealt with it in about six months, with any luck)! Instead, I grabbed my pocket dictator and dictated a letter to Mr. Rich on the spot, indicating some words I thought his readers might enjoy. In cases like this, my transcriber types the letter and sends it to me on a diskette; I copy it onto my hard disk and then send it. The item never goes on a to-do list.

Paper and Pencil Still Work

If you already suffer from too much technology, there's a simple system that will keep you on top of goals that support your priorities. It works surprisingly well. Simply go to your nearest office-supply store and buy one of those washable wall charts or an oversized set of monthly calendars in cardboard stock or paper. Mount your calendars on the wall and use magic markers, washable felt-tip pens, sticky-note pads, gold stars, red seals, or what have you to represent what you want to accomplish by when. This isn't news to you if you work in an office where any number of people, vehicles, or goods need to be scheduled for optimum efficiency. On a personal basis, such *calendar plotting* works well; you're the boss of the calendar. Moving self-stick notes around is a one-second maneuver. High tech or low tech, do what works.

The Least You Need to Know

➤ Everyone needs reinforcement. Join others who have similar priorities and goals. Develop supportive rituals; report to someone; visualize your success; set up a series of small rewards.

➤ Telecommuting may be the biggest time-saver of your career.

➤ Create a superlong to-do list and split it into short- and long-term tasks.

➤ A low-tech approach has its charms. Calendar wall charts are easy to use and re-use.

Chapter 7

You Won't Miss the Money— You'll Always Miss the Time

In This Chapter

➤ The dangers of doing too many things yourself

➤ You can always make more money; you can't make more time

➤ Trade time for money: Take a taxi or have dinner delivered on occasion

➤ Get a helper who can handle almost anything you need to get done

Americans traditionally have had a streak of rugged individualism within them, typified by John Wayne's movie roles. *He* took care of everything himself. Unfortunately, life is not a movie.

In the workaday world, you frequently see middle managers who attempt to leapfrog several positions in the company by taking on more projects, even though they're already working beyond optimal capacity. Among entrepreneurs, you may encounter someone trying to crack a new market—even while juggling several other balls, short-changing his or her health to keep that circus going.

What are some danger signs that you believe you have to do it all yourself? Consider these symptoms: You think you'll be able to overcome obstacles by working longer; you tell yourself (or worse, your boss) that you "appreciate the challenge." If the people around you think it can't be accomplished, all the better; you'll wow 'em by doing the

Warning
Watch out if you start believing that you alone are the only one who can handle things. Many organizations tend to seek out people with such urges. No one but superheroes need apply.

impossible, right? You might become overbearing with others, but hey, you're in pursuit of an important goal and *that's* what counts. Besides, you're the "only one who can do the job."

Certainly, working hard in itself is not a problem unless you maintain preposterous ambitions or let force of habit push you beyond the point of diminishing returns. If you're willing to stay late, work on weekends, and minimize your vacation time, you just may be your organization's star performer—hey, what a great deal for them!—but too many career achievers fall into an endless cycle. These people feel their accomplishments are too small or too few; they experience disappointment, frustration, and health-threatening stress. To relieve these feelings, they work harder in the hope they'll accomplish more and a golden rainbow will appear.

You Can't Do It All, and You Can't Hide It!

The notion that you *and you alone* must take care of everything is, in a word, erroneous. If working too hard is a way for you to gain the respect of others—or self-respect—it's time to rethink your whole approach.

What a Concept!
Admit to yourself that you can't do everything; acknowledge that trying harder *may not be worth it.*

Some do-it-all people may be egotistical, or trying to be "good enough" in their own eyes by constantly proving their supercompetence to everyone else. If they never quite prove it to themselves, they live in dread of being found out as imperfect.

➤ Rather than focus on your weaknesses, accentuate the positive! Develop your strengths. Also give yourself realistic time frames for ambitious goals.

➤ Divide and conquer. Take smaller steps when setting larger goals so that you don't burst a spleen along the way. When progress is slow, try an alternative route, a new door, or a different mindset.

Penny-Wise, Pound-Foolish

Especially when it comes to domestic tasks, do you get stuck in a miserly mode? Do you think that if you spend a few minutes here and there taking care of this and that you can handle all you seek to keep up with—*and* avoid shelling out the money to have others do it? Many people do.

Each time you avoid getting a service professional, helper, or part-timer—when such parties could aid you considerably—*you're ensuring that you won't win back your time.* Each time you mow the grass, for example, when you don't enjoy doing it, you add to the cumulative total of undesirable tasks in your life (as discussed in Chapter 2). Besides, you're incurring all that unnecessary tissue-and-decongestant expense during hay fever season.

You Can Always Make More Money: You Can't Make More Time

When I make presentations to groups around the country and explain the value of shelling out a few dollars to preserve your time, invariably someone asks, "What do I do if money is tight?" I don't presume for a second that you have loads of discretionary cash stashed away in a trunk somewhere. (Remember, most people spend more than they have.) It's not likely that you have excess greenbacks lying around.

Let's look at hiring others from the vantage point of your life's big picture. You have things to accomplish that can perhaps make you much more money than the $15 you pay somebody to cut the grass.

If you're an entrepreneur or self-employed, it pays to rely on outside services so you can focus on what you do best and make the overall business prosper. If you work for an organization, there are still countless opportunities for relief; you *can* rely on others (at work and away from work) to alleviate the piddling tasks you don't enjoy doing. Thus you can be at your best, get noticed by superiors, and stand a better chance of getting those raises and promotions.

Go!
It makes perfect sense to pay a high-school kid $15 to cut the grass if you can't stand cutting the grass. In the long run, you won't miss the money and you'll be glad you're no longer cutting the grass.

Etched in Stone
You need to be rested and alert when you head into work. Having others take care of domestic tasks helps you in your professional career.

A Little Money Goes a Long Way: Good Money/Time Trade-Offs

It's surprising how common the do-it-all urge is. Nanci Hellmich, a reporter for *USA Today*, uncovered some of it when she interviewed me for two articles. The first appeared in November 1991; in it Nanci invited readers to write to *USA Today* and discuss their time-pressure problems. Several lucky readers would benefit from my counsel (aw, shucks). The second article would include the results of my counseling.

Over several weeks, Nanci received hundreds of letters; she selected respondents for me to call. From the *USA Today* offices in Arlington, Virginia, I had lengthy conversations with a female attorney and a graduate student, among others.

The attorney was perpetually racing the clock, getting her daughters to school in the morning, seeing her husband off on his (frequently long) business trips, plying her trade as a partner in a successful law firm, picking up the children, driving them to various after-school activities, making dinner for them, reading to them, and putting them to bed.

After listening to her story, I asked her why she didn't give herself the liberty of ordering dinner a couple of times a week rather than making it all the time. She said she'd never thought about it, and on first hearing it seemed a little extravagant. I asked her how much she earned. It was considerable. I asked her how much her husband earned. It was more than considerable.

"Okay," I replied, "between the two of you, you're clearing nearly $200,000 a year. Suppose once, God forbid, you had Chinese food or pizza or chicken delivered to your home now and then—and didn't cook at all on those nights. How much would it cost you, once a week, to have dinner delivered?" She thought about it and said, "Maybe an average of $12 a week, so that's $600 a year."

I said, "Would it be worth $600 a year if once a week, particularly during hectic work weeks, you had dinner delivered instead of making it yourself? Would that free up some of your time? Would you enjoy it? Are you worth it?" She agreed on all counts. It's food for thought.

Hitting the Books

The graduate student I spoke with also had a hectic schedule. Besides taking several courses, she worked in the afternoons and was a volunteer for a service organization two nights a week. Frequently she found herself getting up in the morning barely in time to catch the bus. This kind of pressure was no way to start her day; yet it had become routine.

I listened carefully to her story and asked, "How much is the bus ride to school?" She said it was $1.25. I said, "How much would a taxi ride cost?" She was aghast. "I couldn't take a taxi!" I said, "Wait a second. How much would a taxi ride be?" She didn't know, so we paused our conversation. She called the closest taxi company and asked about the charges from her apartment to her class in the morning. The cost was approximately $3.50.

When she called me back, I asked her the million-dollar question: "How upsetting would it be to your budget if occasionally when you were running late you permitted yourself to hail a taxi and pay $3.50 instead of paying $1.25 for the bus?" She thought about it and said, "Well, I suppose occasionally it wouldn't hurt."

I said, "You're right. You could hail a taxi as often as once a week, and in the course of a fifteen-week semester you're only paying an extra $33.75 for the luxury of not being enslaved to the bus schedule. You could easily blow $33.75 on stuff all the time. Why not be gentle with yourself? Acknowledge that you're handling a lot in life right now, and occasionally you deserve to take a taxi ride to school." She relented.

I'll Take Manhattan

If you're a big-city career-type, the same principle applies. If you're up on East 68th Street in Manhattan and have to get down to 39th in a hurry, once every week or so, it won't put a memorable dent in your pocketbook to take a taxi rather than the subway or bus. It costs you $6 more per week, and in the course of a year you're only paying $300. How many times have you blown $300 in ways that were far less beneficial to your overall health and well-being?

What a Concept!

How many times do you get stuck in a miserly mode, pinching pennies here and there, while blowing triple digits on items of marginal value?

Taking the Leap

What time/money trade-offs might make good sense in *your* situation? Consider a few:

➤ **Grocery delivery:** Many supermarkets and grocery markets will deliver for a nominal fee of five to seven dollars. Some offer catalogs from which you can order by phone or by fax. For items you buy frequently, you can establish a standing order whereby every week the market delivers eggs, milk, whatever. You can still shop for new or specialty food items now and then, lugging all those bags home so you remember what it's like. It will reinforce your inclination to use grocery delivery services.

➤ **Office supplies by phone and fax:** Those giant superstores appearing across the planet—such as OfficeMax, Staples, and Office Depot—have delivery service and publish large supply catalogs (with "800" numbers so you can reach friendly attendants who will walk you through ordering). The catalogs also contain "800" fax numbers; you can fax in your order without even talking to anybody. Most vendors deliver at no extra charge if your order is above $50. The orders usually are delivered the next day, right to your door. It's fast, accurate, and painless.

➤ **Gift wrap it, please:** If you're buying presents and the store offers a wrapping service, pay the extra dollar and have them wrap it. Do you particularly want to fiddle with wrapping paper, tape, scissors, string, bows, and all that stuff? If you do, fine, that's your option. For another dollar (or whatever it takes), however, isn't it worth it to have that chore completed?

➤ **Online services:** Rather than doing it yourself, consider the online service vendors who maintain bibliographies, citations, dossiers, and indices for a fee. Sure, software can help you navigate the Net. Extracting what you need, however, takes time—*your* time—your *valuable* time. You can easily instruct a service provider to glean things of interest to you, provide them key words and phrases, and pay the fee for it. (See Chapter 12.)

➤ **Pick-up-and-delivery services:** Get in the habit of using vendors and suppliers who come right to your door. I use one firm that recharges my laser printer's cartridge for about half the price of buying a new cartridge every time.

➤ **Shopping services:** There are people who can go shopping for you to buy gifts for others, new shoes, or nearly anything. Before you snicker, consider: If you dislike shopping (or aren't too good at it) and someone you trust *is* good at it, this could make sense. The professional shopper can actually save you money. He or she knows where to get the best buys. Often the overall cost of the item-plus-the-hourly-fee is less than you would have paid (especially if you often hunt for items in five or six stores and end up paying full retail price).

The Maid Brigade and Other Wonders

In a previous book, *Marketing on a Shoestring*, one recommendation I made to entrepreneurs was to look for local service providers. The Maid Brigade, for example, was the service I used when I wanted to have an office or house cleaned quickly. Rather than hiring a service that sent over a cleaning person or two and required three or four hours to get the job done, the Maid Brigade would send six or eight people at once and finish the job within 45 minutes.

Here are other types of services that probably exist in your community (they'll be called something else in your city, of course).

➤ The Butler Did It (a catering service)

➤ Everything But Windows (housecleaning)

➤ Rent a Dad (house repair when there's nobody around who can drive a nail straight)

➤ The Tree Doctor (tree- and hedge-trimming)

➤ Jumpin' Jack Flash (pick-up and delivery)

➤ Walkin' the Dog (takes care of Pooch when you're gone—or when you're not)

➤ Gutters-R-Us (clears your gutters, saves you from roof duty)

➤ Shake a Leg (airport shuttle service)

There are numerous types of part-time workers as well; some may be more suitable to your needs than others. These include part-time regular employees, temporaries, students (high school, college, and grad school), retirees, foreign-exchange students, and interns from colleges.

You probably can find a bright, motivated student to help you. Schools are full of intelligent, perceptive young men and women, many of whom are seeking an opportunity to gain some real-world experience. Their part-time status doesn't mean they're less intelligent or effective. Many can take a "divisible" unit of work and do a bang-up job on it.

What a Concept!

Most communities have high-school juniors and seniors who'd be thrilled to work for $5.00 an hour—which is above minimum wage. This might not seem like a lot of money to you, but it may to them.

What could helpers do for you? Fair question. Take a look.

What Helpers Could Do for You

❏ Route/sort the mail.

❏ Answer requests for information.

❏ Send out mailings of any sort.

❏ Serve routine customer needs.

❏ Make deliveries and pick-ups.

❏ Survey customers and their needs.

❏ Keep track of necessary data and news sources.

❏ Type mailing lists.

❏ Type *anything*, for that matter.

❏ Keep things tidy, clean, and in good repair.

❏ Study competitors, their literature, and their products.

❏ Make first-round or lead calls to prospective customers.

❏ Hunt for a product or service you need.

❏ Catalog new information or products.

❏ Proofread or double-check anything written.

❏ Track inventory or arrange displays.

❏ Do anything that a less-essential part-time employee could do without excessive guidance.

Identify all those non-essential-but-bothersome tasks you've been putting off and that a part-timer can handle.

Word Power
Seed work is the sort of task you can easily assign to another because the downside risk if they botch the task is negligible.

Seed work functions best when it's a distinct *unit* of work—easily assigned to someone else. For example, suppose you want information on the eight other local companies in your field. A high-school student can easily open the phone book or a local trade publication, visit the sites, write for the brochures (using his/her home address), and summarize the information gathered. A more experienced employee could spot trends or innovations from this data, all with a minimum of your time spent on instruction.

Ten Steps to Finding All the Help You Need

Whether you live in a community of 25,000 or 1,025,000, there are many service providers who can help you with domestic as well as business tasks to free you for whatever makes the most money for you.

By now, you're probably all excited about the prospects of bringing such providers into your life. Good. If you start using such helpers in a systematic way, you'll be far along the road to winning back your time.

Here are 10 suggestions for putting your service system in place:

1. Identify all the tasks you don't like to do. Make this list as long as possible. Be honest with yourself. Separate the list into domestic and career-related tasks.

2. On two separate pages (one for domestic and one for career-related tasks) create a matrix listing these tasks down the left-hand side of each page. (There's an example Task Matrix lurking nearby in this chapter.) Across the top of each page, leave room for four columns; label them **Option 1** through **Option 4**.

	Option 1	Option 2	Option 3	Option 4
Task A	_____	_____	_____	_____
Task B	_____	_____	_____	_____
Task C	_____	_____	_____	_____
Task D	_____	_____	_____	_____
Task E	_____	_____	_____	_____
Task F	_____	_____	_____	_____
Task G	_____	_____	_____	_____
Task H	_____	_____	_____	_____

3. If you list eight tasks down the left-hand side of the page for your domestic sheet, with four option boxes across the top of the page, potentially you have 32 cells to fill. Fill even half of them and you'll be in great shape.

4. Within the blank cells, write down every alternative you can imagine for not doing tasks you don't enjoy doing. You may find yourself writing down such options as delegating the tasks to your kids, your neighbors' kids, or someone you found in a shopper's guide or the Yellow Pages.

Go!
Every time you successfully use one of your many helpers, you're winning back your time!

5. Take stock of your grid. If you don't have good options for some of the tasks, it's time for some fieldwork. Go to your local library, supermarket, or community center and read the bulletin boards. Often you'll find business cards or small ads posted by local entrepreneurial talent. Start collecting these leads.

6. Talk to your local librarian. Talk to the job placement officer at your local high school, community college, or university. Ask around. You're likely to get many names of people who can help you.

7. Consider running your own advertisement. A small classified ad in a suburban shoppers' newspaper will probably cost you less than $6. Go ahead, splurge!

8. Start calling potential helpers (or better yet, get your seventh-grader to make exploratory calls for about $2.50 an hour; you won't miss the money).

9. Interview, interview, interview. Over the phone is fine, in person is better. Map out what you want done; break in your helpers gently, but systematically.

10. Start a file of the literature or information you've collected on all the different types of helpers you've been seeking and talking to.

11. Once you have a file of helpers, keep adding to it, keep it current, and use it.

The Least You Need to Know

➤ You drop tons of money all the time on stuff that provides little benefit compared to the time savings you can readily enjoy once you get out of your miserly mode.

➤ Among the best time/money trade-offs are occasional taxi rides; delivery of dinner, groceries, and office supplies; and any other vendors who pick up and deliver.

➤ A wide variety of service providers can help you. They advertise in suburban "shopper" newspapers, on library bulletin boards, and at odd places around town.

➤ High-school and college students can help you enormously, part-time. Many are ready, willing, and able; with some, the only drawback is that they're young (if they learn fast, that's no big deal).

➤ Create a grid of all the domestic tasks—and then all the career-related tasks—you'd rather not be handling. Then identify as many as four options for each task.

➤ Create an up-to-date file of key literature and information you encounter when seeking service providers; constantly add to it. Align your life with people who can free up your time. You're worth it.

Part 2
Taking Charge of Your Turf

Armed with all the great stuff you learned in Part 1, undoubtedly, you're now ready to kick some derrière and stand up for yourself—first by lying down *longer and more often, as in sleep. You're not sleeping enough, bucko.*

Once you're well rested, you can better handle everything that everyone is asking you to do. Not just your boss—family, friends, and neighbors may tend to ask more of you simply because you can do it. So you need some carefully-thought-out excuses.

If you can reduce requests for your time, you'll finally be able to tackle your office and desk. (A desk, you know, is not a filing cabinet; window sills and the corners of your room are not permanent storage locations.) Then you can learn to manage piles and trials with smiles, and investigate some low-cost technology that won't drain your brain to use. When you make it to that point, you'll learn clever ways to handle all the messages that have been bombarding you.

Let's begin with an eye-opening look at why you're hardly able to stay awake days and (too often) find yourself up all night.

Chapter 8

Getting Sleep: As in "Spreading Out Horizontally"

In This Chapter

➤ Most people are not getting enough sleep

➤ Can you really catch up on your sleep?

➤ The impact of too little sleep on your effectiveness

➤ How to get more rest throughout the day

You're not getting enough sleep. If my guru-powers were fully perfected, I'd gesture hypnotically and give you eight full hours of sleep before you read this chapter. (For now, I'll have to let you continue reading.) How do I know you're not getting enough sleep? It's not a lucky guess; study after study shows that most American adults have been gypping themselves of the proper amount of sleep they need.

The director of Stanford University's Sleep Center says that "most Americans no longer know what it feels like to be fully alert." A *Prevention* magazine survey showed that 40 percent of U.S. adults—more than 71 million people—"suffer from stress every day of their lives and find that they can sleep no more than six hours a night."

Short-changing your sleep on any given night (provided it's only one) won't cause you any harm. Most experts agree that getting only three to four hours of sleep once a week is not likely to result in long-term problems. You might feel crummy the next day but you can compensate by taking a nap or going to bed early the next evening.

How important, however, is sleep to you in your quest to win back your time? How important is it to your overall health and effectiveness? (Hint: highly, extremely, incredibly, all of the above. Choose one.)

To Sleep, Perchance to Dream

In *The 24-Hour Society*, Dr. Martin Moore-Ede found that repeatedly having less sleep than you need, day after day, can lead to actual disaster. Moore-Ede contends that George Bush's collapse during his visit to Japan, Captain Joseph Hazelwood's ineffectiveness in piloting the *Exxon Valdez*, and a rash of plane, train, and other transportation mishaps can all be traced back to insufficient sleep on the part of those in question.

How much do *you* need to sleep each day? It all depends—for some people, seven hours a night is great; for others it's eight; for others, nine. Most adults need about eight. College students may need an average of nine to nine-and-a-half hours (whether or not they stayed up till three in the morning, they'd still *need* more sleep than a 35-year-old).

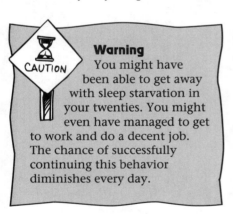

Warning
You might have been able to get away with sleep starvation in your twenties. You might even have managed to get to work and do a decent job. The chance of successfully continuing this behavior diminishes every day.

As people age, some need more than eight hours a night, some need less.

Dr. Jack Eddinger at Duke University's Sleep Center says that "the older one gets, the less smooth one's sleep pattern. It is normal for someone between 40 and 70 to be awake some part of the night." As you age, you may need *more* than eight hours of sleep nightly if it's punctuated by wakeful periods (not uncommon).

You've long known that you need to get enough sleep to function effectively. Yet you probably haven't been getting it. Who, or what, is the culprit? Here's a lineup of the usual suspects.

Adhering to Ritual

If you've gone to bed at eleven for the past several months, chances are you'll go to bed around eleven this evening. If you just have to turn in around the time *Letterman* is over, you've developed a *habit of retiring late*.

Alternatively, if you have magazines, newspapers, compact discs, and all manner of things to read and hear surrounding you, it's tempting to stay up yet another twenty or thirty minutes—which can balloon into forty to sixty.

If you're among the lucky who doze off as soon as you begin reading, thank your stars. Many people stay up longer when surrounded by information stimulants.

Energy Depleters

If you use drugs (especially alcohol), your sleep patterns will be disrupted and you're likely to get too little sleep. Alcohol might knock you out faster, but it can cause sleep difficulty and frequent wake-ups.

Relying on Compensatory Mechanisms

Your eyes may be open, but don't let that fool you. Moore-Ede found that many people engage in *microsleep* (the body's attempt to compensate for under-sleeping) throughout the day. For example, microsleep can occur when:

➤ Bus drivers have full passenger loads.

➤ Truck drivers are racing down hills hauling nuclear weapons.

➤ Mothers transport their babies.

Drowsiness comes in waves. You can be alert one moment, drowsy the next, and not know the difference. Having too little sleep the night before (and certainly on an extended basis) increases the probability you'll engage in microsleep.

> **Word Power**
> **Microsleep** is a five-to-ten-second episode where your brain is effectively asleep while you are otherwise up and about. Microsleep can occur while you are working at a PC, or (omigosh) driving your car.

Disrupted REMs

You've probably heard of REMs—*rapid eye movements* that are a crucial part of your overall sleep cycle.

If you sleep too little or are awakened at inopportune moments, your REM pattern can be disrupted; hence even eight hours in the sack may not yield the benefits of a solid eight hours' sleep. *To win back your waking time, protect your sleep time.* May I suggest the following?

➤ **Don't sleep with your head by a telephone that can ring aloud.** Remove the phone from your bedroom, or install an answering machine and switch the ringer from "on" to "off." Too many people sleep with their heads by the phone because they have aged loved ones far away; they worry about that *one* call in fifteen years that might haul them out of bed at 3:00 a.m. *Stop doing this*; there's not much anyone can do at that hour. You'd be far better off getting fifteen years of sound sleep.

➤ **Once a week, get to bed by 9:00 p.m. Your body will thank you.** Let yourself go to dreamland for nine, ten hours, whatever it takes. Remember, you're probably going to live longer than you think you will—to get to old age with grace and ease, allow yourself at least one weeknight in which getting sleep is your only objective.

➤ **One Friday night each month, crash right after work and don't get up until the next morning.** Have dinner or skip it, as suits you. If you want to experience a fabulous weekend, this is the way to start.

➤ **Avoid caffeine for the six hours before retiring.** This means if you're thinking about going to bed around ten, four in the afternoon or before is the last time to imbibe any caffeine. But hey, why drink this drug-in-a-cup anyway?

➤ **Avoid alcohol in the evening.** Sure, it'll put you to sleep quickly, but it tends to dry you out and wake you up too early. Then you have trouble getting back to sleep, your overall sleep time is reduced, and the quality of your sleep is poor.

➤ **If you fall asleep when you read in bed, then do so to induce drowsiness.** Don't overdo this. Dr. Eddinger says it's important to make your bed and bedroom for sleeping (and, of course, sex) only. Don't set up your bed as a command station with your CD player, TV, or other appliances that reinforce the notion of your bedroom a place for anything *but* sleep.

➤ **Go to bed when you're tired.** Let your body talk to you. It'll tell you when it's tired. The problem you've had in the past is that you have ignored the message.

➤ **Don't fret if you don't fall asleep right away.** You may need a couple minutes or more. After 30 consecutive minutes of restlessness, do something else until you're tired again.

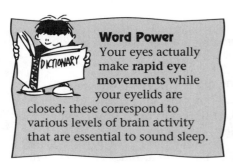

Word Power
Your eyes actually make **rapid eye movements** while your eyelids are closed; these correspond to various levels of brain activity that are essential to sound sleep.

➤ **If you're kept awake by your spouse's snoring, or you're the one snoring, you need help.** I recommend a snore-control device available from The Sharper Image. Whenever your snoring is above a certain decibel level, you receive a gentle vibration which breaks the pattern and helps you return to quiet sleep.

➤ **Moderate exercise several hours before sleep aids in getting sound sleep.**

➤ **Moderate intake of proteins, such as a glass of milk, also aids in sound sleep.**

Can You Really Catch Up on Sleep?

The answer is yes *and* no. No, from the standpoint that if you've been gypping yourself of sleep for the last three years, you can't literally add back all the hours you missed. That kind of "catch-up" sleep won't support the continuing need you face each day.

What a Concept!

Even if you've gypped yourself of sleep for a prolonged period, if you devote the next month to giving yourself all the sleep you can get, you'll be in reasonably fine shape.

Nevertheless, your body is extremely forgiving. Ex-cigarette smokers know this. Even lungs abused by years of smoking begin to cleanse themselves once the smoking stops for good. The effects of ten years' abuse can greatly diminish in as little as one year. So it is with chronic undersleeping.

Habit-Forming

Getting enough sleep, like engaging in other healthy practices, is a habit. Albert Gray, a successful businessman of yesteryear, said, "Every single qualification of success is acquired through habit. Men (and women) form habits and habits form futures. If you do not deliberately form good habits, then unconsciously you will form bad ones."

To be honest about it, gypping yourself of sleep *is* a bad habit. Yes, I know all the excuses and rationalizations. Of course you have a lot to do. No one will debate that. You'll get it all done more effectively and more efficiently with sufficient sleep, not with less sleep.

Here are several suggestions to develop (or perhaps redevelop) the habit of getting sufficient sleep:

➤ Let others know about your newfound quest—this means family members who might otherwise impede your progress.

➤ One weekend day per month, linger longer in the morning before getting up. Some people call this "sleeping in."

➤ Any time you're traveling for work, try this trick as a reminder: Give the TV channel changer to the front desk at the hotel. You can't afford to be still clicking away at midnight. Get sleep when you're on the road (more on this shortly).

➤ Schedule extra sleep any time you're on vacation as well. An extra thirty to forty-five minutes can make all the difference in the perceived quality of your vacation.

➤ Recognize that at first you may have to force yourself to get into bed, especially if it's 9:00 or 9:30 on a weekday evening and you'd rather be up and around. Consider: The opportunity to get precious sleep is too good to miss.

You may have to break the flow of your normal evening activities to get that sleep. Next time they start to make claims on your time, consider them as if they were traffic. I

Go!
Get to bed early *tonight.*

remember, at the end of a workday years ago in Washington, D.C., heading west on M Street to get to Arlington: There was absolutely no break in the traffic. There I was in my car, trying to take a left; literally eight minutes went by without an opening. I concluded that *no opening would be provided*—no matter how patient, respectful, or needful I was. I was going to have to make my break and take the opportunity. You have to take the opportunity to get the rest you need. You're in the driver's seat.

Too Little Sleep and Your Effectiveness

In *The Organic Clock*, Kenneth Rose says that each part and function of your body is timed. Each has its own rhythm—heartbeat, breathing, speaking, even hiccuping. If you sleep too little for too long, you disrupt well-developed cycles that took millions of years to evolve.

Rose also found that every bodily function has internal controls for its basic rhythm. Each body function is reset every 24 hours to parallel the natural light cycle of the day. You are subject to this *circadian rhythm*. Trying to alter that rhythm for a prolonged period can be contrary to your own physiology. *Your body won't like it.*

If you find you can't sleep more even when you try—or seem to need almost endless amounts of sleep—it may be an indicator of depression or another clinical problem. See a physician in this case.

For proper functioning, you need to get the right amount of sleep most days. When you are sleep-deprived, you incur changes in brain waves and literally cannot be as effective. Your immune system and mental skills decline. In *The 24-Hour Society*, Moore-Ede found that certain times of the day *are especially important to sleep through*. Human physiology is

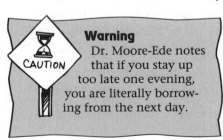

Warning
Dr. Moore-Ede notes that if you stay up too late one evening, you are literally borrowing from the next day.

at its lowest level of alertness between 2:00 and 5:00 a.m. Highest alertness is between 9:00 a.m. and noon, and 4:00 to 8:00 p.m. Your alertness will vary according to hours of consecutive work, hours of work in the preceding week, your regular hours, the monotony you face on the job, the timing and duration of naps you take, lighting, sound, aroma, temperature, cumulative sleep deprivation, and much more.

How Much Sleep You're Probably Getting

I'd guess that your sleep deficiency ranges between 35 and 75 minutes daily. If you're deficient by more than 10 hours a week, as a rule it'll take you about a month to "re-cover." Again, this doesn't mean you can "replace" all the hours you've gypped yourself. It means, instead, that you *can* get to the point where you're fully functional and mini-mize (maybe eradicate) the effects of past deprivation. To get there, start at Square One: a list of indicators that you're probably not getting enough sleep. Some of these may be familiar; some may represent news:

➤ You bump into things more frequently than is normal for you.

➤ You slur your words.

➤ You have trouble digesting food.

➤ You're short with people when normally you wouldn't be.

➤ Your eyes are tired.

➤ Your *joie de vivre* is missing.

➤ You don't enjoy sex as much as you used to.

➤ You need to wake up by alarm clock (many people wake up when they want to, on their own).

➤ You don't want to face the day.

➤ Even small tasks seem to loom larger.

➤ Your life has achieved a level of fine monotony.

➤ You find it easier to engage in tasks that don't involve talking to others.

➤ As much as you hate going to the dentist, you find leaning back in the dentist's chair rather relaxing.

➤ You find yourself nodding off in what are otherwise interesting and/or important meetings.

➤ You "zone out" for unknown periods of time while working.

How Much Sleep You Need

Only you can determine how much sleep you need. I know I've had all the sleep I need when I'm ready to bolt out of bed in the morning, ready to face the day. I recognize it as a signal that I'm well rested. To determine your optimal sleep time, consider the following:

➤ Experiment with the number of hours you sleep each night for a week. Start with eight hours, say 10:30 p.m. to 6:30 a.m.

➤ If eight hours feels good, stay right there; no need to move on. If not, *increase* the amount by 15-minute increments.

➤ If you're waking up before you've slept eight hours (and you're not napping excessively during the day), perhaps you need less than eight. (More on naps in a moment.)

➤ To make your test valid, give up your alarm clock! Yes, give it up (any time you can afford to—not, of course, when you have a plane to catch). Any time it wakes you up, you don't truly know how long you would have slept.

If you have the opportunity, taking naps throughout the day, (even the weekday) can enhance your overall effectiveness and put you in the driver's seat of winning back your time.

The Art and Science of Taking a Nap

Some people nap without problems; others can't nap at all. One study found that if you nap for 30 minutes each afternoon, you actually have a 30-percent lower incidence of heart disease than people who don't nap at all—such a deal. Napping increases your alertness for the rest of the day. Although many people feel a little groggy for a few minutes after a nap, it gradually subsides and you're more alert (and in a better mood—try it).

What a Concept!

The extra edge napping provides can last for 8 to 10 hours. So if you can steal one, you could be good for hours!

Warning

Don't use naps to catch up on sleep if you habitually short-change yourself each evening. It doesn't work.

Short naps are actually more productive than long naps. A short nap will leave you refreshed, whereas a long nap may interfere with your sleep that evening. The experts say that the best nap time is between 2:00 and 3:00 p.m. Any later and your nap may be too deep, interfering with your nightly sleep. If you can, nap in a bed or cot but not a chair. Your quality of sleep will be much higher and the immediate benefits more apparent. The only caveat: *Naps are not a substitute for the proper amount of sleep.*

Is It Sleep or Is It Dehydration?

Hydration and dehydration play an important role in how much sleep you need.

About half the time I feel tired during the day is because I haven't taken in enough water. Nutritionist David Meinz of Norfolk, Virginia, says every chemical reaction that occurs in your body requires water. In fact, your brain is 75 percent water.

Meinz says that your thirst mechanisms lag behind your true need for water on a continual basis. Even a two-percent reduction in your amount of body water will render you less productive than otherwise. A five-percent reduction can seriously decrease mental functioning. Here are Meinz's suggestions for ensuring you're sufficiently hydrated:

➤ Eight cups of water a day is still the standard, but don't wait until your thirst reminds you that you need water. Drink before you're thirsty.

➤ If you work out a lot, it takes your body a full 24 hours to regain the water supply that you need. Hence, you have to have much more water than you think when you work out.

➤ Try drinking eight ounces of water before starting your workout. During your workout, drink as often as you can.

➤ Sign on with the best water-delivery service in your area or buy bottled water. The best choices for bottled water are distilled water or spring water.

➤ If you continue to use tap water, let it run about 30 seconds so any sediments can clear out.

Word Power
When you're **hydrated**, your body's tissues are sufficiently filled with water. To be **dehydrated** is to be parched.

Meinz also says to take a multivitamin every day to reduce feelings of lethargy and to ensure that you're getting most of the basic nutrients. Along with sufficient water intake, this will help you feel more vibrant more often during your day.

Five Ways to Get More Rest Throughout the Day

In addition to previous recommendations, here are seven other ways you can get more rest throughout the day without putting a dent in your overall output:

1. Find a quiet place in your office, an empty conference room, or a coworker's office where you can simply sit in a chair for a few minutes and be still without fear of interruption. Even two or three minutes in a semi-reflective state can help regenerate your batteries.

2. Go outside to a bench, your car, or some other safe haven where you can do the same.

3. Don't bolt right away from the table after eating your lunch. Linger for an extra minute or two; give your food a better chance of being properly digested.

4. Rest while you walk. This sounds like a contradiction, but you can walk *hurriedly* or *restfully*. On your way back from the restroom, a coworker's office, or lunch, stroll mindfully down the hall in a rhythmic fashion, fast enough that no one will accuse you of being a zombie, but sufficiently slow that you're hardly exerting yourself. This can work wonders.

5. Practice the same restful habits outlined here on Saturday and Sunday as well as during the week. Who says you have to go all out during the weekend? Obviously the opportunities for outright naps are much greater on Saturday and Sunday, so take them.

What about when you're feeling drowsy but you have to be awake and alert? In that case, think light and cold. With bright lights, your sense of alertness is enhanced and your brain is switched on. In essence, brightness equals wakefulness.

If your office or workspace is somewhat on the chilly side (say, 68 degrees or less), you're also likely to stay more attentive and alert. As a rule of thumb for making presentations, it's better to have an audience cold and awake than warm and sleepy.

Getting a Good Night's Sleep, on the Road

You know the scenario. You're bedding down for the night in a hotel and need a good night's sleep so you can summon enough energy to hold your own at the meeting the next day. Unluckily, the guest from hell is in the next room and apparently is trying to break the decibel barrier at 2:30 a.m. Normally you're a sound sleeper, but this time you find yourself awake a good four hours before you intended. What can you do after checking into your hotel room to make sure you get a good night's sleep every night, regardless of sleeping accommodations (or lack of them)?

You Can Always Call the Manager

Noise is invading the room you've rented. If it's easy enough to determine the direction of the sound and the intrusion is from the room to the left or right, you could try tapping (gently but firmly) on the wall. This alone sometimes works. In many hotels, the phone system allows you to readily dial adjacent rooms. If the noise is from across the hall or above or below you, you could call and ask the night manager to handle the situation.

And a Gadget Shall Lead Them

To maintain greater control of potential sound disturbances, there are some essential items to have in your possession before checking into any hotel room: A "sound screen," earplugs, and a timer.

1. **The Sound Screen® is a portable white-noise device developed by the Marpac Corporation.** The Sound Screen emits different frequencies and amplitudes of a droning, non-disruptive blanket of sound. You can use this device to minimize the effects of startling or disruptive sounds outside your room. By placing the screen about 10 feet from your head in the direction of any disruptive noise, you are able to minimize the intrusive effects immediately.

2. **Create your own white noise.** If you're awakened and the offending noise isn't too outrageous, use an empty channel on your TV set or radio as a white-noise machine. If you're using a TV this way, turn the brightness down to nothing or cover the entire set with a blanket or towel to minimize light from the screen. If it isn't bolted down, put it between you and the noise. Experiment with your room's thermostat. Perhaps you can turn on the fan (or the heating or cooling system, depending on the season). Use the ventilation system as a white-noise device; adjust the number of blankets and sheets you need accordingly.

Space-age earplugs called Noise Filters® are available from the Cabot Safety Corporation (listed below). They cost little and weigh even less. Airline gate and runway crews (employees who guide planes to and from their gates) use these industrial-strength plugs to shut out heavy-duty noise; they can provide you with a near-silent world. The plugs expand in your outer ear canal, blocking out sound in ways traditional earplugs cannot. Here's where you can get these godsends:

> **Word Power**
> A **sound screen** creates a sound "barrier" that breaks up, masks, or mutes the effects of louder sound from beyond the barrier by using **white noise** (a sound much like that of rushing water).

Noise Filter®
Cabot Safety Corporation
5457 West 79th Street
Indianapolis, IN 46268
Phone (317) 872-6666

Sound Screen® and Sleep Mate®
Marpac Corporation
P.O. Box 3098
Wilmington, NC 28406-0098
FAX (919) 763-4219

3. **Use a timer.** The third essential device is your own alarm clock or timer. You can wake up on cue and be free from having to keep your room phone plugged in.

When you remove the plug from the phone, be sure to position the cord so the end is exposed to you; it will remind you to plug it back in when you get up.

How to Know You're Well Rested

If you're committed to getting back to the level of sleep and rest you need—and are looking forward to being more awake, alert, and refreshed during the workday—you're already well on the way to making this happen. While you'll *feel* the difference, nevertheless here's a checklist of indicators that let you *know* you're getting the amount of sleep you need.

➤ You look forward to facing the day.

➤ You no longer need an alarm clock to get up.

➤ You awaken with energy, feeling great.

➤ Your eyes look clear, not red and bloodshot.

➤ You put in a full workday and have a deep-down satisfaction about what you've accomplished.

➤ You have sufficient energy for activities after work as well.

➤ You look forward to sex.

➤ Your *joie de vivre* is back.

The Least You Need to Know

➤ Within a month, you can largely recover from a prolonged pattern of insufficient sleep. Get started tonight.

➤ Insufficient sleep has a heavy impact on your effectiveness. Don't pretend otherwise.

➤ Safeguard your sleeping area by removing the phone, converting your bedroom back to a room where sleep is what primarily occurs, and so on.

➤ You may need to take a nap during the workday, or at least practice one or more methods of getting brief rest. You *definitely* need to drink more water.

➤ One indication that you're getting enough sleep is bolting out of bed in the morning without having to use an alarm clock.

Chapter 9

I Can, Therefore It's Asked of Me, or (Worse) I Volunteer!

In This Chapter

➤ What to do when your boss wants you to be a workaholic

➤ How to defend your calendar

➤ How to say no with grace and ease

➤ How to get off and stay off mailing lists

The ever-growing array of widely available office technology affords you the opportunity to do far more in a day than your predecessors of yesteryear. Concurrently, it also gives your boss and organization the opportunity to get more *out* of you and expect more *from* you. You used to be able to generate a handful of letters each day if you were lucky. Now, with a few keystrokes, you can crank out 1,000 letters and still have time to be totally exhausted before the end of the day.

The great paradox of today's work environment is that the more you can do, the more is expected of you. Unfortunately, expectations about what you can accomplish rise

Warning
You don't want to be an office wimp—a routinely unsung hero who's requested (or is that *commanded*?) to perform great feats of productivity simply because you can—with no regard to your personal well-being and personal balance.

immediately with the introduction of tools that facilitate greater accomplishment. This explains why you frequently feel squashed in the gears of your worklife like a '90s version of Charlie Chaplin in *Modern Times*. Instead of working on a real assembly line with which you can't keep pace, your "assembly line" is digital, byte-sized, and cyber-driven at nearly the speed of light.

You know you're a good worker. You're only too happy to help your organization in meaningful ways. Unfortunately, not all organizations make meaningful demands.

Let's explore how to further take charge of your turf and win back your time starting with the vital challenge of managing your boss.

Managing Your Boss

There have been whole books written on this subject! Fortunately, I'm going to encapsulate them for you into the following single sentence:

> *Ultimately, you'll be treated by your boss in the way you teach your boss to treat you.*

There, I've said it. A gross oversimplification? Look around your organization. Who gets stepped on the most? Who is handled with kid gloves?

Generally, the office wimps get used as doormats, and those who are a bit more particular as to how their workday unfolds are treated with at least a tad more respect. The key to not having your boss consume the time in your life beyond the normal workday involves re-examining the issues discussed in Chapter 1 and learning some specific phrases that you can offer as needed. Read on.

What to Do When Your Boss Wants You to Be a Workaholic

Hey, it happens. You've got this great position in this great organization; there's only one itty-bitty little problem—your boss is a workaholic and expects you to be the same. This situation requires great tact and professionalism since you're not likely to change your boss's nature. You are likely to be confronted with his or her workaholism and its effect on you. Here are some key phrases that might help unstick you. (They work even better if your boss is *not* a workaholic!) Commit these to memory; in many cases it's essential that your retort be automatic.

➤ "I'm overcommitted right now, and if I take that on I can't do it justice."

➤ "I appreciate your confidence in me. I wouldn't want to take this on knowing my other tasks and responsibilities right now would prohibit me from doing an excellent job."

➤ "I'd be happy to handle this assignment for you but realistically I can't do it without foregoing some other things I'm working on. Of tasks *a* and *b,* which would you like me to do? Which can I put aside?"

➤ "I can do that for you. Will it be okay if I get back to you in the middle of next week? I currently have blank, blank, and blank in the queue."

➤ "The number of tasks and complexity of assignments I'm handling is mounting. Perhaps we could look at a two- or four-week scenario of what's most important to you, and when the assignments need to be completed, versus what I can realistically handle over that time period."

Even workaholic bosses are appreciative of your efforts on occasion. When the boss knows that you naturally work hard, he or she is not as likely to impose on you so often. A great time to make a sterling effort is when the boss is away. Most people follow the old adage, "when the cat's away, the mice will play."

It behooves you, therefore, to be the one who's able to go into the boss's office after he or she returns and say, "Here's that big report you wanted. It's all done."

When the boss is outside of the office, perhaps on travel or simply downtown on appointments, that's when he or she is most likely to monitor who's doing what back at the office. That's when the boss calls in more frequently, inspects things a little more closely upon returning, and is more on-edge, knowing that most employees tend to slack off. Hence this is your chance to shine, teach this workaholic that you don't need to be motherhenned, *and* make great strides toward controlling your time.

Go!
If you're the one who works hard when the boss is away, you help to convey a message that he or she doesn't need to constantly keep heaping on assignments.

Defending Your Calendar

It's a strange phenomenon—when you look at your calendar months in advance and there's nothing scheduled, that's when you fall into time-traps. Suppose Jim comes in and asks you to volunteer with him, three months hence, for a charitable cause he supports. You open your appointment book or look on your scheduling software and see there's nothing going on that day. So you say, "sure, why not?" You mark it dutifully on your calendar. You even intend to honor your commitment.

Two months go by. As you approach the date on which you promised Jim you'd volunteer, you notice that you now have responsibilities in and around it. A day or two before the time you're supposed to help Jim, your schedule is jam-packed. Suddenly, Jim's long-standing request looks like an intrusion. How dare he! Yet, when he asked and you agreed, it all seemed so harmless. All of which leads to *Jeff's Law of Defending Your Calendar*—which states (among other things):

> *An empty calendar is not such a bad thing.*

Why are you inclined to schedule tasks, responsibilities, and events for which you volunteer, but aren't inclined to schedule leisure-time activities, particularly those on a weekday after work? Hopefully, you have no trouble scheduling a vacation. What about scheduling calendar-pockets of fun, leisure, and relaxation throughout your week? You need to defend your calendar on a continual basis.

Whoa, I'm not saying that volunteering to help someone isn't worthwhile. It may be highly worthwhile. On the heels of 5,000 other things you have to do, however, it may not be appropriate for you to take on another task at this time.

Your life, as discussed in Chapter 1—your career, year, month, workweek, and day, are finite. If you are similar to other professionals, your calendar is your life—therefore you need to defend it.

Warning
If you don't defend your calendar, it will surely be filled in with all manner of "worthwhile activities."

As an exercise, I suggest you go back through prior years' calendars and examine the appointments, activities, and tasks that you entered back then. You'll gain perspective on how many things you scheduled that you could've done without. In reviewing my own prior calendars, before I got all this wisdom, I observed that 40 to 50 percent of my activities were nonessential. Some could've been cut given my knowledge of their results. Most however, could be cut simply because they weren't in accordance with my priorities and goals. I yielded to the whim of the moment, or I hadn't developed the ability to say no.

Avoid and Win

Here's a quick list of techniques to help you determine whether you can safely avoid adding some future commitment to your calendar:

➤ Is it in alignment with your priorities and goals?

➤ Are you likely to be as prone to say yes to such a request tomorrow or next week?

➤ What else could you do at that time that would be more rewarding?

➤ What other pressing tasks and responsibilities are you likely to face around that time?

➤ Does the other party have other options besides you? Will he or she be crushed?

➤ Do you like him or her?

➤ If none of the above work, make your decision in three days hence, particularly when you can respond by phone, mail, or fax. It's much easier to decline when no one is physically before you.

Learning to Say No with Grace and Ease

There is a direct relationship between the size of your organization and the number of requests you receive to attend or support various functions. If you're an entrepreneur, a student, or retired, you still are likely to face a number of requests, the brunt of which are best handled with a polite "no." With Joe's retirement party, Sally's baby shower, Aunt Millie's sixty-fourth birthday party, the Little League parade, and who knows what else, it would be easy for you to fill up your calendar and never get your job done, let alone do the things you *want* to do in life.

You don't need to bone up on volumes of Amy Vanderbilt, Letitia Baldridge, or Miss Manners to be able to say no with grace and ease. If you simply learn to employ any of the following responses as they apply, you'll be in great shape:

➤ The easiest technique you can use to decline a request is to say that your child's birthday/recital/graduation/sex-change operation will be occurring at that time, and you couldn't possibly miss it. This is not a lie; undoubtedly your child will be doing something that merits your presence.

➤ Closely related is anything your *family* has planned. For example, "Oh, that's the day our family is taking our annual fall foliage trip. We've been planning it for months, and the hotel reservations have already been made. I do appreciate your asking, however."

➤ You may be able to work up enough guts to say, "You know, I'd like to, but I'm so overcommitted right now I couldn't work it in and do it justice... or be fully attentive... or offer the level of support that I know you'd appreciate."

➤ "I wish you had asked me a couple of days ago. I already committed that time to helping XYZ accomplish ABC."

➤ "Could I take a rain-check on that one? I've been working myself to a frazzle lately and I've scheduled that time to be with my... therapist... masseuse... mistress... bookie."

If you have no legitimate prevailing circumstances, here are other possible responses:

➤ "Let me get back to you by tomorrow on that..." Tomorrow, use the aforementioned phone, mail, or fax to politely decline.

➤ Offer a gently-worded "Thanks, but I'll have to pass on that."

➤ The wimpish approach (but hey, it might work) is to use the conditional "no." "If Joe Smith (from across the country) doesn't ask me to do XYZ, then I may be able to." Later, tell them that Joe *did* ask you.

Reducing the Info-Glut

You face so much that competes for your time and attention—your workaholic boss, overfilled calendar, and future commitments. So you'll need to think in terms of controlling the number of demands coming at you. Don't volunteer to have others hit you with even more that will compete for your attention. Do you open your intellectual kimono willy-nilly and permit newspaper, magazine, and newsletter publishers to sign you up?

Warning
Without thinking, do you add your name to mailing lists, thereby openly surrendering yourself to more data and more deluge?

The effect of all this is having too much to respond to, feeling overwhelmed, and having no sense of control over your time. The next time somebody calls with a highly worthwhile publication you can subscribe to, use what you've learned in this chapter to politely decline. In addition, the following techniques for handling magazine subscriptions may be of use to you:

➤ As each of your magazines subscriptions expire, don't immediately renew. Wait two to three months to see if you actually miss having the magazine. If you don't, then you've saved some money and a whole lot of time. You can always view several issues at a local library. Most importantly, recognize that in a society in which information flows abundantly, no particular magazine (unless it's highly specialized) is that crucial to receive anymore...

➤ If, however, you do miss it, then resubscribe. The publication will take you back, I promise—in many cases you'll even get a better rate.

➤ For the magazines you do receive, immediately strip them down; tear out or photo-copy only those articles or passages that appear to be of interest to you. Then recycle the rest of the publication. (More on this in Chapters 11 and 12.)

➤ One of the great benefits of having an online service is the ability to quickly peruse articles from dozens of publications, download and save them on hard disk, and read them at will—without ever having to handle paper at all. After reading them, you can wipe them off your disk or keep them. Either way, you avoid glutting your physical systems—filing cabinets, desk drawers, and file folders.

➤ For existing subscriptions, experiment with giving away every second or third issue. Even chemists, engineers, and highly technical types agree they could skip every third issue of their technical publications and be no worse off; most periodicals have an inherent, built-in redundancy.

➤ Many magazines publish a roster of all the articles that were run during the year in their final publication of the year. Such indices can be invaluable; you can highlight exactly which articles you would like to see.

➤ Some publications maintain a readers' service whereby you can order only the articles you desire.

Getting Off and Staying Off Mailing Lists

By extending the principles of reducing your magazine glut to your mail, you ultimately can save even more time. To get off and stay off mailing lists write to the addresses listed here and ask to be removed from the list. Those organizations represent some of the most formidable mailing lists in the U.S.

Junk-mail organizations:

Advo Inc.
> Director of List Maintenance
> 239 West Service Road
> Hartford, CT 06120-1280

National Demographics & Lifestyle
> List Order Services
> 1621 18th Street #300
> Denver, CO 80202-1294

Donnelley Marketing
> 1235 North Avenue
> Nevada, IA 50201-1419

Equifax Options
Equifax Marketing Decision System
P.O. Box 740123
Atlanta, GA 30374-0123

Mail Preference Service
Direct Marketing Association
P.O. Box 9008
Farmingdale, NY 11735-9008

Metro Mail Corporation
901 West Bond Street
Lincoln, NE 68521-3694

R.L. Polk and Company
List Services Division
6400 Monroe Boulevard
Taylor, MI 48180-1884

Trans Union
Transmark Inc.
555 West Adams Street
Chicago, IL 60661-3601

Some strategies follow; you can use them to ensure that your name's removed from the mailing list(s). Some of them may seem like a lot to do. Once you get rolling, however, the peace of mind and time savings you reap from having less junk mail cross your path will be well worth the effort!

➤ When you write to them, include all variations of your name, such as Jeff, Jeffrey, Jeff Davidson, Jeffrey P. Davidson, and so on, and all others in your household for maximum effectiveness.

➤ Thereafter, write to them at least once every four months with a follow-up reminder; any purchase you make by credit card or check is likely to get your name back on the direct-mail rolls.

➤ Create a printed label that says:

"I don't want my name placed on any mailing lists whatsoever, and forbid the use, sale, rental or transfer of my name."

➤ The Direct Marketing Association in Washington, D.C., has published a pamphlet entitled, *Direct Marketing Association Guidelines for Ethical Business Practice;* it offers a comprehensive review of your rights regarding unsolicited third-class mail. For example, consider Article 32 on *"List Rental Practices."*

Under the heading "Use of Mailing Lists" the DMA states "consumers that provide data that may be rented, sold or exchanged for direct marketing purposes periodically should be informed of the potential for the rental, sale, or exchange of such data." It further states, "list compilers should suppress names from lists when requested from the individual." To reach the ethics department of the Direct Marketing Association write to this address:

Ethics Department
Direct Marketing Association, Inc.
11 West Forty Second Street
New York, New York 10036-8096
(212) 768-7277
FAX (212) 768-4546

➤ When you are besieged by third-class mail from repeat or gross offenders, and such offenders have included a self-addressed bulk mail reply envelope, feel free to use the envelope to request that your name be removed from their lists. Also, review their literature to see if there is an 800 number by which you can make such a request, at no cost to you.

➤ For those who do not heed your request, lodge a complaint with the Direct Marketing Association or the U.S. Postal Service.

➤ Sometimes the fastest way to deal with repeat offenders is to simply write the words "Speed Reply" right on the communication from them that you've received, and underneath those two words write this message: "Please remove me from your mailing list now and forever." Sign your name, date it, and send back the very items or communication that you received. Be sure to address it to the mailing list manager of the offending organization.

➤ At all times and in all places, inform the parties with whom you do business that you do not appreciate having your name added to a mailing list and being inundated by catalogs, announcements, brochures, fliers, and so forth. This is particularly necessary if you place an order by fax, make a purchase by credit card, fill out a magazine subscription form, or procure any other type of good or service other than by cash.

As an extreme measure, I once carefully wrapped up a brick, and on the outside of the wrapper included this note to a gross offender: "I respectfully request that you remove my name from your mailing list. This is my eighth [or whatever number] request, and if unheeded, I shall send 10 bricks next time." After wrapping up the wrapped-brick-and-message, I affixed the bulk-mail-postal-reply face of the envelope sent to me in the latest mailing. I taped it securely to the package and dropped it in a mailbox. Technically, of course, the post office didn't have to deliver it (I'd defaced the reply envelope), but the delivery went through. It seems I made a dramatic, costly impact on the original mailer, who then chose to heed my request and eliminate my name from their rolls. (They called me and surrendered.)

By now, you may be thinking "this guy's got a vendetta against junk mail." I don't. I have a vendetta against waste—all the time wasted in relation to the delivery of mail I never wanted to receive in the first place.

What a Concept!

The less unwanted mail you receive, the more time in your life. Period.

The Least You Need to Know

➤ At all times, if you have too much scheduled, too many commitments, or too much to read, remember who invited all that hassle into your life: You.

➤ If you have a workaholic boss, you'll have to memorize key statements that you can spring at appropriate moments.

➤ Defending your calendar is synonymous with controlling or winning back your time. Beware particularly of future commitments. They get vexing as their time draws near.

➤ Practice saying no with grace and ease, in front of the mirror or with family members. Use legitimate reasons (such as your kids, family, or prior commitments) so you can thank the other person for asking—but then respectfully decline.

➤ Manage your magazine subscriptions. Keep your name off of mailing lists.

O.K. GANG
JUMPIN' JACKS!!

Chapter 10

Whipping Your Office into Shape

In This Chapter

➤ Managing your desk and guarding the flat surfaces of your life

➤ Quick and easy ways to handle paper

➤ Use self-stick labels and long-life stampers for maximum advantage

➤ What to chuck and what to retain

On the road toward taking charge of your turf, you've learned two major principles thus far. In Chapter 8, you read about the dramatic impact sleep can have on the quality of your life and your effectiveness, both on the job and off it. In Chapter 9, you saw some ways you volunteer (perhaps unwittingly) to have more assignments, commitments, and information thrown your way—and that it's possible to keep much of this at bay.

Now it's time to tackle the vital notion of whipping your office into shape. You can rule an empire from a desk if you know how to do it correctly. Too many people treat their offices and their desks with benign neglect.

Deskmanship for Fun and Profit—
Taking Charge of Your Desk

Have you seen the movie *Top Gun*? Tom Cruise plays a Navy fighter pilot. Among his many responsibilities in flying some of the nation's most expensive aircraft is landing Navy jets safely on aircraft carrier decks.

A few months after seeing the movie, I was read an article in the *Smithsonian* magazine about how aircraft carrier decks have to be completely clean and clear before a plane can land. "All hands on deck" on an aircraft carrier deck means that everyone, even senior officers, pick up a push broom and sweep the deck completely clear when a plane is due to land. The goal is to leave nothing on the surface of the deck, not even a paper clip, to ensure the highest probability of a successful landing. What happens if there is debris on the deck as a plane approaches? Or—oh boy—an earlier plane has not left the landing strip? The approaching plane is likely to crash and burn.

What a Concept!

Your desk, gentle reader, is like the top of an aircraft carrier deck. If you take the next pile of stuff you get and simply park it in the corner of your desk with some vague notion that an organizing fairy will come by and do something with it, good luck when the next thing lands!

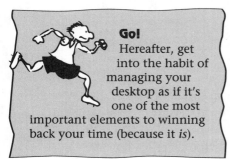

Go!
Hereafter, get into the habit of managing your desktop as if it's one of the most important elements to winning back your time (because it *is*).

Nobody's coming to help you to manage your desk; each new item you pile on will (figuratively) crash and burn in the smoldering ruins of the accumulations in progress.

All other things being equal, if you have but one project, one piece of paper—whatever you're working on—in front of you and the rest of your desk is clear, you're bound to have more energy, focus, and direction for that project. Conversely, if all manner of distractions compete for your attention—piles of reports, memos, and faxes— how can you have the same focus, energy, and direction on the task at hand?

What Do You Keep on Top of Your Desk?

What to keep on top of your desk is uniquely individual. As a general rule, anything you use on a daily basis (such as a stapler, roll of tape, or pen), gets to stay on top of your desk. Remove anything you can safely remove from your desktop. Where does it go? You might have a credenza behind you. In case you're thinking, "Well, you asked me merely to shift my stuff from one surface to another," you're right. And it works.

Inside your desk, retain items you use at least weekly if not daily—but don't start storing supplies there. Those belong further away from you, in file cabinets or supply lockers. Your goal is to maintain the optimal number of items on and in your desk: enough so you work efficiently every day without cluttering up the works.

> **Etched in Stone**
>
> When it's behind you, it's not in front of you. Consequently, you're not facing it all at once—not watching it sit there being "too much to do."

After you've cleared your desk of what's unnecessary, apply the same principle to the top of your filing cabinet, closet shelves, and other aspects of your life. What about your dining room table, or the trunk or glove compartment of your car?

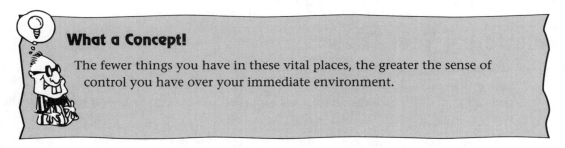

What a Concept!

The fewer things you have in these vital places, the greater the sense of control you have over your immediate environment.

Your goal is to have about what you need, and not much more. Oddly enough, once these flat surfaces are under control, you also gain a heightened sense of control over your time. Such a deal!

Staying in Shape in Front of the Computer Terminal

Time out for a quick aside to computer users. Because you sit at your desk so often, for so much of your work day, in many instances facing the monolithic computer monitor, here are a few tips (assembled from various office equipment manufacturers) for overcoming the sedentary inclinations that facing a PC tends to propagate:

➤ Breathe in slowly through your nose, holding it for two seconds, and then exhale through your mouth. Repeat this several times and you'll likely experience an energy boost.

➤ Roll your shoulders forward 5 or 6 times using a wide circular motion; do the same thing backward.

103

➤ Turn your head slowly from side to side and look over each shoulder. Count to three. Repeat the exercise 5 to 10 times.

➤ While in your chair, slowly bend your upper body between your knees. Stay this way for a few seconds, then sit up and relax. Repeat this once or twice to stretch your back.

➤ Hold your arms straight out in front of you. Raise and lower your hands, bending them at your wrists. Repeat this several times; it stretches the muscles in your forearms and gives your wrists relief.

➤ Fold your arms in front of you, raise your elbows to shoulder level and then push them straight back. Hold this for a couple of seconds. This gives your upper back and shoulder blades some relief. Repeat 5 to 10 times.

Also, take a break now and then. By working more effectively with this piece of office equipment, ultimately you get more done. If you do even a few of these exercises, you'll feel better about your time during the workday and afterward. Another beneficial side effect: you'll probably be more effective.

Mastering Your Shelves

Ah, shelves! What an invention. Do you ever consider what goes on a shelf versus what goes in a filing cabinet? Since filing is the subject of Chapter 11, let's focus on the first part of the question here; what goes on your shelves. In a nutshell, your shelves are the home of

➤ Items you're bound to use within the next two weeks.

➤ Items too large for a filing cabinet (or collections of like items).

➤ Projects in progress.

➤ Supplies that can go in supply cabinets.

Let's examine each of these individually.

Items You're Bound to Use Within the Next Two Weeks

These include reference books, directories, phone books, manuals, instruction guides, books, and magazines (especially large ones, annual directories, and theme issues).

Collections and Items Too Large for a Filing Cabinet

Because it's difficult to file some thick items such as books (and some magazines) in a filing cabinet, any such item is better housed on your shelves. Any oversized item that simply won't fit in a file cabinet (and any item that is part of a continuing series) is probably best housed on your shelves.

If you receive a key industry publication and it makes sense for you to hang on to back issues, these also belong on your shelves. In this case, you could acquire magazine holders—essentially precut or preassembled boxes (corrugated cardboard or plastic) that hold about 24 issues of a monthly magazine. The box itself enables you to stay in control. It's visual; you can stick a face-up label on it. It's easy to grab one issue from among the many you're retaining; it's easy to replace the issue.

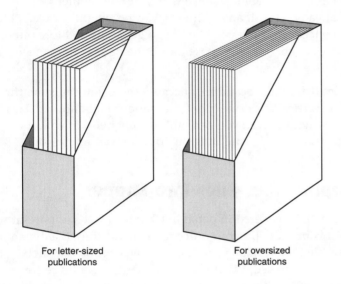

For letter-sized
publications

For oversized
publications

Cardboard magazine holders help you stay in control of incoming items.

Projects in Progress

Similarly, if you're working on a project that requires a variety of items, the magazine boxes work well. If you keep your shelves behind your seat at your desk, keep one shelf compartment clear so you may lay incoming file folders flat upon it. You'll have a way station for new stuff while keeping your desk relatively clear. The prevailing principle is that it's better to have these materials *behind* you than right in your immediate work area. Undoubtedly you face many demands during the day; you may have to draw upon several folders for different projects or tasks. It makes sense to have a single flat surface (even among your shelving units) readily available to accommodate active files.

> **Warning**
> You *could* employ stacking trays, but they tend to become semipermanent collections of paper rather than projects in progress.
>
> CAUTION

Supplies—Which Go in Supply Cabinets

Most professionals today have *no* difficulty in one activity: filling up their shelves. Every supply catalog, Chamber of Commerce directory, or new software manual consumes a few inches of precious horizontal space.

Warning
More shelves are seldom the answer to keeping your office in shape.

Your inclination might be to get more shelves, but it would be best to avoid that. Your goal is to keep your office in shape within reasonable parameters—using the desk, filing cabinet, shelves, and supply cabinet you already have. If any of these is always overfilled, okay, I'll concede: *perhaps* you need to go get another. More often, lack of space is an excuse for not being able to manage an office.

Keep supplies in a supply cabinet (isn't logic beautiful?) because there you can store them in bulk. Stack them horizontally, vertically, or one type of item on top of another. Treat your *shelves* as somewhat sacred; align them so you can pull out key items at will. If it takes you longer than thirty seconds to find something on your shelves, refine your system.

Advance Word on Whipping Your Files into Shape

While "filing for fun and profit" will be covered in detail in Chapter 11, it's important to look at the relationship between your files and your office in general. Filing is a dynamic process. Items you place in your file folder today may find their way onto your shelves, re-emerge in some other form, or be chucked. What's on your shelves may (in some mutant form) find its way into your files. If you have a big reference book on a shelf, you may have to extract a few pages from it, discard or recycle the larger volume, and retain only a few essential pages in a folder in your filing cabinet. The relationship among all your storage areas is dynamic; your prevailing quest is to boil down what's crucial for you to retain—keep only the essence.

Information is power; if you can't find what you've retained, it's of no value to you. Worse, the time you took to read and file the items would then be wasted.

Go!
When something is discardable, let it go.

Are you fearful about tossing something because you just *know* you're going to need it tomorrow? Chapter 16, "The Urge to Merge and Purge," will help you here. Suffice to say for now that *if there are no discernible downside consequences to tossing something, toss it.* Most of what you're retaining is readily replaceable anyway. Office efficiency experts claim that 80 percent of what executives file, they never use again. Even if that's only partially true, it still means a significant chunk of what you're retaining is deadwood.

To the degree you can clear the deadwood out of your desk, files, and office, you keep your office in shape. That enhances your capacity to properly handle what else comes in (and you read Chapter 3; you *know* more is coming). It also raises the probability that you'll find those items you actually need.

Consider the cumulative time savings you could chalk up whenever you look for something. That's probably 12 minutes saved per day, minimum. That adds up to an hour per week and fifty hours per year. That's like creating an extra week for yourself. As a kicker, those in your office get a clear message that you're someone who is able to remain in control, find things quickly, and stay on top of situations. Hence you get a multiple payoff for keeping your files (and your office in general) in shape.

What a Concept!

The great paradox of engaging in housekeeping activities is that getting things in shape takes time. But don't give up. The small time investment you make in developing your newfound efficiency will pay off over and over again down the road.

Handling Paper

Even with the advent of the PC, the fax/modem, e-mail, and downloading online files, paper is still the dominant means of communication and the scourge of your career. The most repetitious task you face, day in and day out, is handling paper. To win back your time is to win the battle with paper.

When you receive a catalog, magazine, or other thick publication, strip it down to its essence. What *few* articles, pages, or items of interest do you want to retain? Once you identify those, recycle the rest and reduce the potential for office glut.

Immediately reduce books, manuals, and long reports to their essence; manually scan the entire document (using your eyes, not a hand-held scanner). Copy the few pages you wish to retain, along with title page, table of contents, and any critical addresses, phone, or fax information. Your goal: retain the few pages that seem important; recycle the larger document.

Go!
Your goal is to get control—and stay in control—of the paper that comes your way.

Let Your Copier Help You

When new items arrive in your office, consider the creative ways you can strip them down to their essence, particularly using the copier. Can you create a single sheet, perhaps front and back, that captures the essence of the larger document? Can you create a single sheet that captures the essence of several small scraps or tidbits you wish to retain?

When I speak at conventions, sometimes I ask the audience members to hold up their wallets. This gets a chuckle, but the exercise is well worth undertaking; if their wallets are thicker than half an inch, they're carrying too much in there.

Lakein's "C" Drawer

Alan Lakein, a management specialist of yesteryear, had a nifty idea about what to do with the mounting piles of stuff you can't deal with just now, but want to review when you have a chance. He suggested putting everything in what he calls a "C" drawer, meaning it's not an "A" or "B" item. You can't chuck it at the moment, but you certainly can't deal with it at the moment.

Warning
When confronted with too many scraps and information tidbits, it's easy to fall into the habit of parking them in your wallet, on your desk, or in your drawers.

In this drawer, you temporarily house what you want out of sight and out of mind. Go back to your "C" drawer when you have the time and strength, take out the items, see what needs to go into your file system (probably not much), what you can immediately chuck or recycle, and what goes back into the "C" drawer. I maintain a "C" drawer and find it helpful, particularly when I'm working toward a deadline and I encounter something that normally I might review immediately. I pop it into the "C" drawer and get back to what I was doing.

Assessing the Paper That Comes Your Way

When you're confronted by yet another report, document, or who knows what, ask yourself these questions:

➤ *What is the issue behind this document?* What does the paper represent? Is it an information crutch, data that you already know? If so, chuck it. Does it represent something you think might be important in the future? If so, put it in the "C" drawer. (See Chapter 11 for a variety of other files you can create to house such documents.)

Often the issue behind the paper flood is, in retrospect, too minor to merit your attention. Sure it looms large at the time, but what doesn't if it arrives in screaming headlines? For years newspapers have been able to sell their wares simply by use of language and font size. The issues addressed often have precious little to do with the typical reader.

➤ *Did I need to receive this at all?* This can be an insightful question to ask yourself. In many cases, the answer is no; that means you don't have to spend another second on the item. Now and then, something you didn't need to receive comes your way and *is* of interest. (Rare, but possible.) Most such items you can chuck immediately.

➤ *How else can this be handled?* Can you *delegate* what needs to be done regarding this new piece of paper? Referring back to Chapter 7 on using helpers, is there someone in your cosmos who can handle this for you and free up your time for more important things?

If no one else but you will do, how else can you handle it so as to have (in good old computer biz-speak) "quick and easy throughput?" Can you fax instead of mail? Can you e-mail instead of fax? Can you pay by check instead of in person? Can you pay by credit card by fax instead of by check? Can you highlight the five items in the important company memo that merit discussion at the next meeting instead of trying to have a handle on all 22 pages?

➤ *Will it matter if I don't handle it at all?* This is a critical question. Much of what confronts you requires no action on your part. For example: announcements regarding upcoming publications, ads that tout prices or services, and anything addressed to "current resident." If you don't pay your rent or your mortgage, you'll be contacted by someone interested in collecting the money. If, however, you don't participate in the office pool, don't attend the local charity ball, don't make an extra copy of that recipe, or don't learn about that software game, your life *will not change*.

Items to Discard

Without equivocation, go through your office on a search-and-destroy mission. Trash anything that fits these categories:

➤ Outdated manuals.

➤ Back issues of publications you haven't touched in more than two years.

➤ Drafts, earlier versions, and outdated versions of letters, correspondence, memos, reports, and documents that have already been produced as final (unless you're in the legal department of your organization; then it's your job to hang on to such—ahem—*material*).

➤ Carcasses of once-useful stuff: dead white-out, dry pens, pencil nubs, or business cards whose vital information is already logged on to your database.

➤ All scraps and tidbits of information, used Post-It notes, and the like that have accumulated around your desk, in your wallet, and elsewhere. Get them on a single sheet or log them into a file on your computer.

➤ Excess vendor supply catalogs.

➤ Manuals you will absolutely never open again.

➤ Outdated catalogs, flyers, annual reports, brochures, promotional materials.

➤ The hoard of thumbtacks, pushpins, pennies, and paper clips that gathers in the corners of your desk drawers.

➤ Take-out/delivery menus from restaurants you never visit (or visit so frequently that you've memorized the bill of fare).

➤ Lingering stacks of irrelevant documents; extra copies of relevant documents. Keep what you need. Discard the rest.

Items to Acquire

There is nothing mandatory for you to acquire. The following items, however, may help you keep your office in shape:

➤ Color-coded file folders, tabs, labels, and long-life stampers (more on these in Chapters 11 and 13).

Long-life stampers can cut down on the time you spend handwriting or organizing material.

➤ Magazine holders for your shelves.

➤ A few three-ring notebooks for storing and maintaining like items.

➤ A mechanical arm that hoists your monitor over your desk. You can use it to bring your monitor closer or move it aside, depending on how much room you need for your work (if your computer's disk drives are in a tower case, you've just freed up a square foot or so of desk space).

➤ A larger wastebasket.

Near your desk—but not *on* it—go the loving and familiar items—pictures, plants, and motivators. Also install any supporting accoutrements (from VitaLites to ocean-wave music, if they support your productivity, efficiency, and creativity) near, but not on, your desk.

The Least You Need to Know

➤ Your desk is among the most important arenas of your life. Take charge of your desk, and you take charge of your time.

➤ Refine your office setup so you can find whatever you're looking for easily. (That's right, *easily*.)

➤ Everyone faces a continuing barrage of scraps and information tidbits. Corral these, copy them all onto a single page or into an appropriate computer file. Do not let them accumulate.

➤ Continually discard what does not support you, and acquire what does. Get ruthless about this.

➤ As often as possible, keep your desk clear of everything but the one task at hand.

Chapter 11

Filing for Fun (!?) and Profit

In This Chapter

➤ Filing becomes even more important as the world grows more complex

➤ Essential tools for mastering this high art

➤ It's both what you file, and how you file it

➤ How a creative filing system uniquely serves the way you work

Do you look upon filing as drudgery? If so, you're not alone! You don't see people shooting movies, writing Broadway plays, or producing hard rock albums on the topic. It's rather mundane, pedestrian, and (shall I say it?) even a tad boring. Yet it's an unheralded key to winning back your time.

As discussed in Chapter 10, when you're in control of your desk, office, files, and the resources you've assembled, you are a more focused, efficient, effective professional. In this chapter, I will focus exclusively on filing. Don't give me that look; it's going to be engrossing, and it'll give you a career edge.

Filing as a Concept

First, it's important to ask the big question: Why file? Here are two big answers:

1. Files have value—ideally, you file items because you believe that. (Most items don't have value, which is why you may regard filing as unproductive.)

2. There are consequences for *not* filing. You save receipts from business expenses so you can be reimbursed by your organization and comply with IRS regulations. Filing tax receipts makes sense—it keeps you out of jail.

If you're in sales, you file information that will enable you to make greater sales in the future. This includes notes on customers and perhaps their catalogs, brochures, and reports.

Warning
Most of what confronts you will have little impact on your career or your life—very little. Therefore most of what crosses your desk is a clog that *dare not find* its way into your files.

Consider everything you have ever filed! Each item presumably had (or has) potential future value, if only enabling you to cover your derrière. Why do people eschew the mere thought of filing? Beats the heck out of me. Maybe they don't see the connection between filing and its future impact on their careers and lives.

Actually starting the process is very time-consuming, but it is one of those necessary tasks that *save time later*. Rather than spend hours searching for an item, you'll be able to find it pronto. So it's well worth a day or two during downtime to create a system that supports you.

A Few Simple Tools

Filing requires only a few simple tools and the proper mind-set. The tools are:

➤ **A chair.** You can file while standing if you have a four-drawer filing cabinet and you're dealing with the top drawer. Usually your filing activity is easier if you're in a chair, particularly a swivel chair. If you're way behind in your filing, you won't want to be on your feet.

➤ **A desk or flat surface.** This comes in handy when you staple or unstaple, paper-clip or un-paper-clip. Often you'll have to mark the folders you insert in your file cabinet, making notes on what you're filing, folding, ripping, or taping together. A flat surface means never having to work in mid-air.

➤ **File folders.** File folders are essential. Rather than the two-cut or three-cut manila folders that have been around since Moses crossed the Red Sea, you can get blue, green, brown, red, pink, black—any color you want. They can be letter-size, legal-size, or have a protruding label area.

➤ **File folder labels.** These can be color-coded as well. You don't have to order the same old white labels. You can easily have subsections within your green file folders by using labels of different colors.

➤ **Filing cabinets with ample space.** The next time you visit your doctor or dentist, ask to see how the patient files are stored. Health-care providers often use a modular stacking shelf system (see the illustration in this chapter) that gives them immediate access to the record needed.

Go!
If you haven't ordered file folders before, you're in for a revelation. Open up any office supply catalog and let your creative juices flow. Colored file folders enable you to stay organized with less work. How so? You can use green file folders for anything that relates to money, red for government, blue for (true blue) customers, etc.

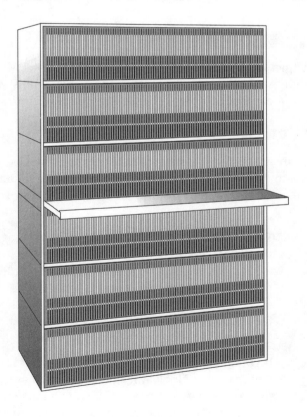

A shelf system like this one provides the room you need to set up any kind of filing system.

➤ **Color-coded dots.** These help you find files quickly, even if you're already using color-coded files and labels. You could put a small red dot on files you anticipate using in the next week or two. The real value of the dots, however, is that you can leave the files in the file drawer instead of on your shelf or desk.

➤ **Staplers, paper clips, and other fasteners.** Keep these on hand; you never know when you'll need to fasten or unfasten items before you file them.

What a Concept!

Unlike the Ten Commandments, what you file is not etched in stone. You can move things around, chuck them, add or delete files…go wild. Your goal for now is to get things into their best apparent home.

Filing Madness—and Sanity

I've touched on these principles in previous chapters, particularly Chapter 10, but now I'll get to the particulars. Suppose you face a mass of items (or is that a mess of items?) on your desk. How would you tackle it? How would you whip that stuff into shape?

This Way to the Ejection Seat

Go through everything rapidly and determine what can be tossed, as well as what duplicate or outdated items you don't need. Some items won't fit in your file folder anyway; it's best to copy the handful of pages you need from them, file those pages, and recycle the rest.

"When in doubt throw it out." These immortal words, uttered two decades ago by efficiency expert Edwin Bliss, are still true. If you're not sure about keeping something, in most cases you've already answered the question: NO. If you're like most professionals, you have a tendency to overfile, which gluts your system and helps hide anything you need to find. If you ever file too much stuff, use the "C" drawer discussed in Chapter 10 as a way station for potential file items.

Go!
If someone does your filing for you, give him or her the next several pages as a reading assignment.

If you question whether to file an item, put it aside for a day or two and look at it again. Often the answer will present itself. Ask yourself, "What will happen if I pitch this?" If there's no significant downside, chuck it gleefully.

Look for Like Items

In that great mass (mess?) of stuff before you, if eight items refer to delegation, that's a clue to start a file folder labeled "delegation." Do the same with other groups of like items.

Wade through the entire pile; toss what you can and group like items together until everything is tossed or grouped. Yes, some items will stand alone. Not to worry.

When approaching each of your mini-piles, ask yourself:

> ➤ Can I consolidate each pile by using the backsides of documents, single-page copies, and shorter notes?

> ➤ Can I consolidate scraps and tidbits by using the copier to create a dossier page or stapling them into a packet?

> ➤ For piles that only have one or two items each, is there a way to group them together? (An article on office chairs might join your notes on organizing your desk in a piled called "office furniture.")

Managing the Mini-Piles

Go through the materials you've put in mini-piles; see if any of them should go into all-encompassing files such as "copiers" or "insurance." Always, *always* seek to have a few large files of like items, not a gaggle of small files. It'll be easier to find what you want in the course of your day, week, year, or career.

Use date stamping if it suits you. Some efficiency experts suggest putting a date stamp on every item you file. If you've been holding on to an item for, say, 18 months and haven't used it, maybe it's time to chuck it.

It's not mandatory to use date stamping; an item's future relevance isn't always linked to how long you've had it. Generally, the longer you've held on to an item, the less chance it has of future importance...*but it ain't always so.*

Customized File Headings

This is the part where filing gets to be fun. (You're laughing. See? I told you.) By using customized file headings, you can devise compartments that enable you to give the materials that cross your desk a jet assist: anxiety-free, guilt-free, and fat-free. For example, if you often don't know where to file items, you can create a file called, "Where to file this?" (I use one called "Check in one month.")

Other handy file names you could use include these:

➤ Read or chuck

➤ Read when I can

➤ Review for possible linkage with ABC project

One profound question you face when you consider filing any item is, "Where does this go?" Your quest is then to find an appropriate file where you can park the item and find it again easily. Often that means relabeling files. That's fine; you're further refining your system, putting your smarts into developing a personal information retrieval system.

Monthly and Daily Tickler Files

You can benefit greatly by creating file folders for each month. Then, when something crosses your desk in December but you don't have to act on it until February, into the February file it goes.

Go!
You're the boss of labeling your files. Get creative with file headings; hone the system until it works best *for you*.

Word Power
Tickler files automatically remind you of when you need to deal with a particular task. When the request for the task hits your desk, you can place it in the tickler file for the appropriate future date. Every day of the month, check your tickler file for that day to identify tasks to take on for the day.

You can have a 31-day tickler file as well. If you receive something on the second day of the month but don't have to deal with it until the 14th, put it in the file marked the 14th, or give yourself some extra time and put it in the file marked the *13th*. (Think about it.)

You can use this system to pay bills on time. Write the checks in advance, sign them, seal them, stamp them, and put the envelope in the appropriate folder of your 31-day rotating tickler file. Review that file at the start of each week and perhaps once or twice during the week; you'll know automatically when it's time to pay a bill or address a date-filed item. (More on this in Chapter 13.)

The monthly files and 31-day tickler files will help you reduce clutter while offering you peace of mind. Simple? Yes. It's also remarkably efficient.

When you view something several days, weeks, or months after first filing it, you often have greater objectivity and a new chance to act on it, delegate it, or toss it. If a lot of stuff gets tossed, fine; at least you had those things out of your way for all that time.

Creating Files in Advance of the Need

Suppose you're planning to go to graduate school for a master's degree. One way to accommodate the growing body of literature you'll be assembling is to create a file folder *in advance of having anything to file.* When stuff comes in that appears worth saving, it'll have a home.

If you're thinking that this is just a way to collect more stuff, won't you reconsider? Creating folders in advance of the need can be a potent reminder and affirmation of your future goals.

Suppose you come across a brilliant article on how to finance your degree in a way that considerably reduces your burden. Where are you going to put that article? Park it on top of something else where it will sit for weeks or months? You still won't know what to do with it, but you'll want to hang on to it—right?

What a Concept!

You can start a new file folder, label it, and park it in your file drawer without anything in it! Yup. Are you crazy to do so? Nope.

What are some files you can create in advance of having anything to put in them—merely because it makes sense, based on where you're heading in life? Here are some suggestions:

➤ Your child's higher education fund.

➤ Your retirement home.

➤ Your vacation next year to Greece.

➤ Assisting your aging parents.

➤ Evolving technology that interests you.

➤ A new medical operation that might help you.

What a Concept!

Woody Allen once said that 85% of everything is just showing up. At least 50% of dealing with all the piles of paper you confront is simply making room for them.

Extending the Principle

Creating a file in advance of having anything to put in it works on a computer hard disk as well. If a new project is about to start or you'll be scanning information on a new topic, why not create a directory for it on your hard disk? I do this when I bring on a new part-time helper.

Go!
You can use this same principle for working with someone else, downloading files from online, or parking items-in-progress.

Suppose Bob is going to start in a few days. The first thing I do is create a directory named "Bob." As the days pass, I move files into Bob's directory so I already have assignments for him. As he takes them on, others develop; I move them to his directory.

I have a directory called "Inprog" that I go to at the start of each day; from there I might move an item to "Bob" or (once it's finished) elsewhere on my hard disk. You get the picture.

Give Your Files Somewhere to Live

I'd like to spend the next hundred pages on the value of housing your files, but there are limits on our time and space, so I'll have to do it in two. Your goal is to keep close to you the items you use frequently; keep rarely used items furthest from you. Much of what you file *won't* be used frequently.

Of course, certain factors—the nature of your work, tax laws, or other regulations—may require you to hang on to a whale of a lot. Whatever you *have to* hang on to—plus what *you want to* hang on to—can be stored away from your immediate workspace. I'm going to take the leap and assume your organization already has systems and procedures for storing files. What about you? Are you hanging on to all kinds of stuff you cannot bear to pitch? Here's a plan of attack:

1. Group like items, put them in a box or storage container, and mark the box with something descriptive like "check again next April," or "review after the merger."

2. Before storing a container, quickly plow through it once more to see what can be removed. This will simplify your task and you'll thank yourself later.

3. Once the box is out of sight, build a safeguard into your system. Put a note in your "April" file that says to review the contents of the box located at JKL.

Take advantage of emerging technology. Sometimes, instead of storing vast volumes of material, you can simply scan it and keep it on disk. Open the business section of your large metropolitan newspaper and you'll see ads for service providers who do this.

Can anyone else in your organization or family harbor such items so you don't have to? If the box holds reminders of some dear, departed one, perhaps the best solution is to rotate it among the siblings—four months a year at your sister Sally's, four months at your brother Tom's, and four months with you. People do this all the time, especially with stuff they know they'll never go through again but can't bear to chuck.

It's easier emotionally to sell your child's baby clothes if somebody wants them. When you sell items and they meet a need, you feel good. Afterwards, when you have to pack up what wasn't sold and give the items to charity, you might not feel as good, even though it's a commendable gesture. Perhaps there's some kind of emotional relief in getting money for the goods, and emotional blockage when you end up giving them away. Perhaps there is a lingering notion, " I should hang on to these items for posterity. Maybe my child, as an adult, might open the box and appreciate them." You'll need to decide the *exact* disposition of your goods before you hold a yard sale.

Warning
When it comes to domestic items, watch out if you decide to have a yard sale. You and others in your family may disagree about what to keep and what to unload.

Paying for Storage?

If the stuff you've boxed is valuable and compact, maybe it makes sense to put it in a safety-deposit box in a bank. If it's voluminous, maybe consider putting it in a commercial self-storage unit (available in most metro areas).

Paying to store materials brings up the issue of what you're retaining. Is it worth it to pay a bank or a company to retain the stuff? If it is, then you'll feel all right about forking over the dough. If it *doesn't* seem worth the cash, you've just found a good indicator that you don't need to hang on to the stuff.

Recycling

An effective way to keep the clamor of pages confronting you down to a dull roar is to watch constantly for what can be recycled. Can you give a report, memo, or article to a key associate or junior staff person whom it will benefit? If so, it's far easier to let go of what you're retaining.

Word Power
When you rent a **self-storage unit**, you get a garage-like space you can cram full of any items you don't need on a daily basis. For example, you may want to store old files in a smaller self-storage unit. See "Storage" in the Yellow Pages to learn what storage options are available in your area.

Can you use the clean back sides of sheets for rough drafts, scratch paper, internal memos, notepads, and hard-copy fax responses? If so, it will be far easier for you to recycle materials that come across your desk. In this case, rather than tossing the page, you're supporting the environment by getting double use out of your materials. All the folders you use are potentially reusable. Label them over again and give them new life. Recycling also gives you a quick and socially acceptable means of dealing with much of the paper and clutter that arrives during the day.

If you don't take control, you're setting yourself up for glutted files, glutted systems, glutted thinking. Rather than winning back your time, you'll be giving it away. You're at your best when you're a lean and mean working machine.

The Least You Need to Know

➤ Filing is a necessary response to working in an environment of continual overload.

➤ When you're in control of your desk, office, files, and the resources you've assembled, you're a more focused, efficient, and effective professional—and you're certainly more in charge of your time.

➤ You may need to change your mind-set about filing—this is an opportunity for you to devise a personal information retrieval system that supports the way you work and live.

➤ The tools for effective filing are still pretty simple. Colored file folders, labels, and dots help you organize what you're retaining. Purchase them with abandon.

➤ Remove anything from your immediate environment that you don't need to encounter for weeks or months.

➤ Be on guard to recycle whatever you can of the stuff that comes across your desk. This will automatically help you win back your time, keeping your files lean and mean.

Chapter 12

Neat Tools That Work—and Up Your Efficiency

In This Chapter

➤ Eliminating guilt and anxiety about what you haven't learned yet

➤ Avoiding technology time traps

➤ Simple, affordable technologies that can help you both win back and manage your time

➤ Choosing scheduling software, calendar systems and organizers, or manual systems

Scores of books have been written about new technology, making the most of your online time, and how not to get left in the dust by all the techno-twits who populate the cosmos.

What if you had only three reasons to adopt a new tool—your work requires it, your clients use it, or it would give you a real edge? You'd determine the latter by talking with industry gurus, reading objective commentary on new technology, and staying alert and open to new possibilities. Personally, I always let a younger person handle a technology issue I'm facing—why should I bother to figure out stuff that a 24-year-old knows like the back of his hand?

In the early 1980s, IBM, Apple, Tandy, Atari, and other personal computer manufacturers launched vigorous campaigns to convince you, and all of us, that buying a computer was essential to our livelihood. They would soon be correct, but they started the hype *years* before it came true.

PCs were supposed to provide instant solutions—today many of us wouldn't think of doing a job without one—yet I'll bet you've never had a day where you simply sat down at the keyboard, tapped a few keys, and presto! your department or business started running itself. In 1995, the powers-that-be perpetrated new, up-to-date hype: getting online and tapping into the Internet was the be-all and end-all. While there's no denying the awesome power of online information and communication services, it's important to keep things in balance.

> **Warning**
> It's easy to get caught in the trap of acquiring some new tool of technology far in advance of your ability to use it, let alone benefit from it.

Look around your office and your home. Have you been caught in the trap of gathering information or acquiring an item far in advance of your ability (or need) to use it? Have you bought any high-tech items in the last two years that have *simply sat there*? I'm talking about hardware and software, instruction manuals, scanners, additional printers, adapters, cassettes, videos, CD-ROMs, phone systems, fax machines, online connections, online products and services, and…more is coming.

> **Warning**
> "Driven by our obsession to compete, we've embraced the electronic god with a frenzy," says Bill Henderson, leader of the Lead Pencil Club. "Soon, blessed with the fax, voice, and e-mail, computer hookups and TVs with hundreds of channels, we won't have to leave our lonely rooms—not to write a check, work, visit, shop, exercise, or make love. We will have raced at incredible speeds to reach our final destination—nothing."

Peter Drucker, the noted sage of management, observed that for new technology to replace old, it has to have at least "ten times the benefit" of its predecessor. I don't know how he arrived at that figure, but who am I to doubt Dr. Drucker? (For that matter, do you have any techie toy that you feel gives you even *twice* the benefit?)

Technology Time Traps

All technology holds the potential to either help you be more efficient, or further slide you into the morass of the overwhelmed. In *Technopoly*, Dr. Neil Postman says the introduction of any new technology brings benefits *and* detriments. Truer words…

Consider the car phone: If you're the parent of three children, it can give you great comfort to call them via car phone after school at, say, 3:30 p.m. Car phones can be wonderful tools. Some models respond to you by voice, confirming the keys you've pressed or the option you've engaged. The newest models offer voice commands that enable you to "Call Joe Smith," "Call home," "Answer the phone," or "Hang up the phone."

Some car phones have built-in fax and data communications so you can transmit from your car. Some connect to your horn and provide a security feature; others allow emergency dialing and dial the police automatically. Nearly all have some type of anti-theft alarm. Some will dial your home or office when an intruder attempts to make a call!

Cellular phones are always sprouting features: volume control, different rings, wider display screens (brightly lit for easy use at night!), speed dialing, speed re-dialing, and one-touch dialing. Lots of little choices.

Warning
The manufacturers, advertisers, and dealers are adept at helping you focus on the benefits—especially in the rare case that you happen to become a world-class expert user of the system they're offering. Make sure, however, that you find some trade magazines (perhaps at the local library) to actually *read* about the downside of acquiring new tools and technology in your life.

What's the Downside?

When you carry a cellular phone in your car, what other (maybe time-gobbling) factors have you added to your life? Consider:

➤ Anybody can reach you *at any time*.

➤ There goes one of the last sanctuaries you had.

➤ You'd better change your brochures and business cards to include your cellular phone number.

➤ If you're on the phone, are you driving *less* safely?

➤ Unnecessary conversations can cost you.

➤ The newfound annoyance of making one extra call before you get there—to make sure that plans haven't changed...

➤ That nagging feeling that your system is insufficient—gotta have more range, more power, less cost per call...and so on...

It seems paradoxical that a device created to make you more efficient or save you time holds nearly equal potential to do the opposite. Here's a gripping view of why this happens.

The Revenge Effect

"The Revenge Effect is the curious way the world has of getting even, defeating our best efforts to speed it up and otherwise improve it," says Professor Edward Tenner of Princeton. He suggests a basic reason for the failure of technology to solve problems: the way machines and people interact. Freeways, intended to speed travel, lead to suburbs as cities sprawl out instead of up; commuting times climb. Computers make it easy to copy and print files, so you end up copying and printing many more files; your "paperless" office fills up with paper.

Tenner wonders what "revenge effect" the virtual world will have, as virtual communities form and real cities may crumble. What will happen when *more than half the country* is online?

You Set the Rules

When you view each new technological tool as both beneficial *and* detrimental, you're in far better position to stay in control of your time. You could purchase a cellular phone, for example, after deciding on some rules of use—such as only making calls to loved ones and for crucial appointments, limiting calls to under three minutes, and not listing your car phone number on business cards or brochures. The crucial element is that *you* define a personal set of rules for using the tool. Your rules can change, but they're *yours*.

What a Concept!

Hereafter, take a look at both the benefits and the detriments of "time-saving" technological tools you use. Even if you never master everything a tool provides, you'll gain still greater benefits from it if you can understand it well enough to eliminate some of its detriments.

Six types of "neat tools" follow. Some represent highly sophisticated technology; some are simple. They all represent great potential ways to win back the time in your life. With your own rules of use, you'll feel better about how and when you use the tool, and avoid potential time traps.

Using Dictation Equipment

If you want to be more productive in your office and make maximum use of your travel time, use a pocket dictator. No, it's not a petty tyrant (provided you use it right); it's a recording device to capture notes, compose immediate thank-you to people you meet, or produce whole books (yes, even this one).

Even if you're already proficient in using a laptop computer for word processing, using portable dictation equipment offers advantages, particularly if you have a skilled staff who can transcribe your golden words. (By the way, transcription can cost as little as $6 to $9 per hour; consider hiring an industrious college student to do it.)

Go!
By using portable dictation equipment, you can *approach your productivity potential*.

Portable dictation equipment allows mobility. You can dictate almost anywhere. Microcassette recorders allow up to an hour of taping on each side. If you compose directly on a word processor you may be able to type between 40 and 80 words a minute. With a little practice, you can dictate 100 to 140 words a minute. When you type while you're thinking, your mind races ahead of your fingers. Many of the ideas and phrases you compose in your mind are lost.

Once you become familiar with how easy these devices are to use (and the pure joy of finishing written items in one-third the time), there is no returning to old ways. With dictating you can write whatever you've wanted to write, but never had time to.

Fear Not!

If you insist that you can't write without being able to visually review what you've written, consider: a good outline is a prerequisite to effective writing—whether it's longhand or any other method. If you are dictating with a good outline handy, you can expand key words to sentences and paragraphs. The pause feature on all portable dictation equipment allows you to gather your thoughts and articulate them in complete sentences and paragraphs.

While dictating the sentence you've just read, I paused three times. When the material was transcribed (by someone with superb typing skills—effective division of labor!) there were no long breaks in the sentence. It takes a maximum of two to four hours to get the hang of efficient dictating.

The World of Fax/Modems

Okay, this example is going to get a little technical, but bear with me; it illustrates the kinds of issues that come with any high-tech tool. What's important about a new gadget is *whether it meets your needs*, not whether it's always the latest. Technology itself is

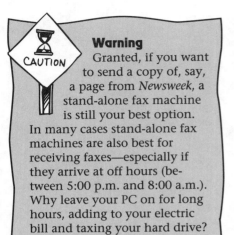

Warning
Granted, if you want to send a copy of, say, a page from *Newsweek*, a stand-alone fax machine is still your best option. In many cases stand-alone fax machines are also best for receiving faxes—especially if they arrive at off hours (between 5:00 p.m. and 8:00 a.m.). Why leave your PC on for long hours, adding to your electric bill and taxing your hard drive?

changing so fast that even my words are obsolete by the time they hit the page. Example: Prices continue to fall for extremely fast dual-function modems. For fifty dollars or less you can add fax capabilities that will help you reduce paper clutter. Sending and receiving faxes from your desktop enables you to store and keep track of them easily. It's easy to index and search transmissions and receptions. Special security features mean no one else is privy to your correspondence. Faxing via fax/modem can save you paper, supplies, time, and money.

If you already have a fax/modem, you know the quality of your fax transmissions is much higher than what you'd get from a stand-alone fax machine. You can log the fax and modem numbers of your recipients onto your software and have your computer dial automatically—a great time-saver—no misdials, *forever*.

If you reach a busy signal, you can set up your fax/modem to redial at timed intervals, the number of times you wish. Fax/modems allow you to change fonts, add graphics, and scan pictures and charts. You can quickly bleep off junk faxes without ever having to handle paper, and easily make a high-quality printout of the transmissions you want to keep.

A fax/modem provides other benefits as well. Its higher transmission speeds can nudge down your overall long-distance charges. You can use it for online searches—the faster you can download information, the greater your savings.

Similar Hardware, Varieties in Software

Most fax/modems feature password-protection, volume control, status displays, phone number storage, rapid dialing, configuration storage, and impaired-line performance (ways to get around a bad connection). As with many technologies, the hardware varies little from one manufacturer to another. The big decisions are price and software.

Warning
Most of the problems you may encounter using a fax/modem are related to improper installation and/or integration between software and hardware.

The market leaders in fax software in the mid-1990s were WinFax Pro for Windows and FaxPro for the Mac. Installed properly, these programs work well—75% of the questions that the software manufacturers receive are on the order of "How do I set this up with my hardware?"

Alas, no technology is perfect. Here are some downside issues you may encounter when you use a fax/modem:

➤ Transmitting a fax while working on something else often slows down your operations, "confusing" the fax software or locking up your entire system. Experts recommend transmitting your fax and then working on something else that is not related to your PC.

➤ If you reboot, fax transmissions start from the beginning, rather than the point of interruption; this is costly and time-consuming.

➤ Faxes formatted before submission by fax/modem are graphical; they require a lot of hard disk storage space. Some users store them for several days to ensure that the recipient received an accurate transmission.

➤ A voice-activated fax machine needs you right there to reply when it says, "If you wish to send a fax, please press the star button now," or "Please start now." Some fax software can respond to this, some can't. You have to monitor your fax transmissions; you can't start a long one and leave for lunch.

➤ If you want to fax, you can't be online! Some advocates suggest installing two fax/modems, so you can simultaneously fax and be online. What's next, four? So you can fax to two people, be online, and download something online? Yipes.

➤ Having a fax/modem may lure you into the trap of oversending. Use a compact cover-sheet, single spacing, and double columns; give the recipient a break.

➤ You have to keep fax/modem transmissions in one font and point size: Courier 10. Every time a fax/modem has to read some fancy font, your transmission slows by double or more and your expense goes up.

When you run into problems, do *not* call the technical support numbers offered by the software developers, even if they're "800" numbers. The call may be free, but you'll end up spending oodles of time on problems you don't need to solve *personally*.

To gain the supreme benefits of using a fax/modem, enlist the techie talent. Unless you have the powers of a supreme computer nerd, *find* one to install, troubleshoot, repair, and perfect your system. Keep yourself free (as discussed in Chapter 7) to do what you do best.

Making the Most of Your Fax/Modem

Here are some suggestions for maximum fax/modem mileage:

➤ Create special forms on your fax software that are smaller than the full 8 1/2"-by-11" page. Shorter faxes mean slightly less transmission time—and the odd size will stand out.

➤ Use special wording such as "Speed Reply" to aid the other party in receiving your fax. (See Chapter 13 for suggestions on using a stand-alone fax machine.)

➤ Keep fax transmissions to *two pages or less* (if it's unsolicited, *one page*). If you're not sure whether you're sending to a stand-alone fax machine or a fax/modem, sending a large document assumes your recipient will receive the entire transmission, *accurately*, and that so many pages won't disrupt their faxing operations. Can you make those assumptions safely?

➤ Unless you have a working relationship with recipients, avoid *broadcast faxes* to everyone and his/her dog. Recipients know instinctively when they are just one of a horde. Such submissions don't tend to generate goodwill.

➤ Include options that help the recipient—boxes or numbered choices that the other party can check off and send back to you.

➤ Use messages such as "important," "urgent," or "read carefully" *sparingly*. (Remember the story of the boy who cried "Wolf!")

Online Services

Unless you've been away on a UFO, you've heard about Microsoft Net, CompuServe, America Online, Prodigy, GEnie, Delphi, and a host of other widely touted providers of online information services. To save your time, I'll simply mention that online services can be a boon for you in winning back and managing your time. All have toll-free "800" numbers; the 800-information operator (800-555-1212) can assist you.

An ever-growing number of information services provide *fax on demand* if you have a fax/modem so you can get the precise information you want, when you want it. These companies include Fortune Company Profiles by Avenue Technologies, Research Reports from Standard and Poor's, and WESTfax from Westlaw (when you're looking for legal documents).

Major online information service providers—such as DIALOG, NewsNet, DowJones news/retrieval, NEXIS, and Dated Times—offer information, reports, bulletins, and clipping services. You can get them via e-mail, electronic folder, fax, or off-line print. To go surfing on the Internet or the World Wide Web (you can look me up at www.brespace.com, by the way), you'll need a graphical-interface *Web browser*.

Ron Wagner, speaker, PC guru, and author of an Internet training guide, says the only Web browser choice that makes sense today is Netscape. Versions are available for Windows and the Macintosh. Stay alert for new developments; the computer scene changes quickly.

The online providers themselves are getting more adept at making their services easier to use. For example, most now allow you to simply type in common keywords such as "bicycles" or "basketball" to zap right over to your arenas of interest. Increasing use of point-and-click icons, menu bars, and truly helpful "Help" commands are now the norm. (It's probably because of all those Windows and Mac users.)

Ancillary service providers such as Individual, Inc. (based in Cambridge, Massachusetts) offer services that work for you around the clock. With its product HeadsUp, you select five to ten important topics for your "time-sensitive information needs." They scan and filter more than 12,000 stories and features from 300 top domestic and international sources—to find the 15 to 20 news briefs of most interest to you. You can choose to receive your information via e-mail or fax. And all this just scratches the surface of the capabilities available online.

> **Go!**
> Articles and features about online services are as close as your local magazine rack: check out *Wired, Mac World, PC Magazine, Information Entrepreneur, Compute, Home Office Computing, PC Computing,* and *Byte.*

Everything Has Its Price...

What's the downside to using online services? Ron Wagner suggests these pitfalls:

➤ You can spend a lot of money in a hurry.

➤ With more people going online to tap into the vast cache of information on the Internet, service providers are struggling to meet the demand; you'll face gridlock— I call it "cyberlock"—on the information highway.

➤ Several-minute waits for online connections are common—and that only gets you connected so you can begin waiting to download information. Often—especially during business hours—you won't even be able to log on to a favorite Internet site.

➤ Once you're logged on, the Internet will put at your fingertips more information than you probably imagined could exist. You'll become more acutely aware of a blizzard of topics you can't keep up with (*no one can*).

➤ You can spend all the time remaining in your life online and, paradoxically, be farther behind than you are today.

➤ You cannot effectively handle more than a tiny *micro-niche* of what's out there. Choose carefully where you're going to spend your time.

➤ When you take in new information, it's difficult to ascertain what is accurate information. Along with the wealth of information you may tap into comes the fool's gold—*misinformation*. Consider *spoof data*, info that's literally a joke. Spoof data is not difficult to create and a few people think it's hilariously funny.

Scheduling Software, Calendar Systems, and Organizers

Here is another area where technology is changing at warp speed. Nevertheless, there are some general principles you can trust.

Warning
Spoof data or not, too often the information you receive is false or inaccurate. Being online hyper-intensifies this risk.

Scheduling software, calendar systems, electronic organizers and the like are often referred to as *personal information managers* (PIMs). Worse, the nomenclature is not standard, some people simply call them *organizers*. I'll call them *electronic scheduling tools* (*ESTs*—my own acronym!).

ESTs are essentially software you load into your hardware, be it your desktop PC or notebook-size computer. Most of these programs offer at least the following basic features:

➤ An appointment-booker calendar

➤ A to-do list

➤ An electronic form of Rolodex

➤ A notepad

On a rudimentary level, you get to store names and addresses, keep appointments on your calendar, record notes, maintain lists, and feel you've *arrived* as an executive. On a more lofty plane, ESTs enable you to identify scheduling conflicts and search through myriad records to zero in on the contact person or information you need. (If you're quite adept at using them, they impress others who see you using them. They think you're working magic; in a way, you are.)

A World of Bennies

Uh-oh! This section assumes very high-level familiarity with computer terms and practices. Much of this discussion is for power-user-wannabes who know the lingo; consult your local guru.

Typical day-to-day use with the best of the ESTs involves generating business correspondence with an integrated word processor and transferring it via e-mail without having to leave your program. Also, you can manage your schedule with a built-in appointment calendar, use drag-and-drop capabilities to move a name and phone number onto or off an appointment calendar, and personalize the way you search and retrieve records.

You can print your calendar or key lists of addresses in hard copy to take with you. You can toggle on alarms, buzzers, or bells to remind you when to make a call—and even have the call dialed for you. A few ESTs allow you to color-code files and bits of information for easy retrieval; the benefits are similar to those of color-coding manual files (see Chapter 11).

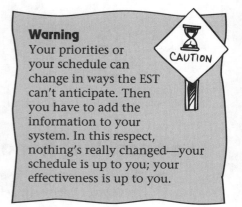

Warning
If you're shopping for an EST, *keep it simple*—identify four or five major features you require. You'll probably screen out most available software products. Give a closer look to the few that make the initial cut.

Some ESTs assist you by automatically completing some fields in your address book when it recognizes keystrokes. If you want to find a carpenter, or someone named Carpenter, or the town Carpenteria, simply type in "Carpenter" and you'll zoom ahead to the first time it shows up. Hit another key and you'll see the second time it shows up, and so forth.

Many ESTs also enable you to insert *icons* on both the appointment calendars and the lists you're maintaining—a flag, a basketball, the sun, a rose, a roller-skate, a star, or some other nifty little picture.

When it comes to price for *any* high-tech tool, keep in mind that *there's always a lower-cost option, but what is the cost of finding it?*

What Can Go Wrong, Will

The downside of using ESTs can be hefty. No EST can reschedule a meeting for you. Anytime you enter incorrect data, "garbage in, garbage out" happens; you'll get the incorrect data back until you fix it.

So what can ESTs add to your life? More organization, some reminders, less clutter, and perhaps peace of mind—if you use them effectively. Of course, that means they have to go wherever *you* go. A variety of providers now offer a *hand-held transfer option* so you can transfer data from your PC to a palmtop. The data exchange is a bit cumbersome now, but soon it'll be smooth and automatic. Other options let you overwrite old data with new information. If a phone number or address changes and you transfer the information between computers, both will carry the correct and latest data. But is it worth the hassle? You'll have to decide.

Warning
Your priorities or your schedule can change in ways the EST can't anticipate. Then you have to add the information to your system. In this respect, nothing's really changed—your schedule is up to you; your effectiveness is up to you.

Other downsides to using ESTs: you may make more entries than you need. Think about how many files you have on your hard disk now—and how many you'll never tap into again. The same pitfall awaits when you begin to use scheduling software. I'll say it for EST files too: keep them lean and mean. Record what you want and need, but have the strength to leave out what you don't. You'll be way ahead and more in control of your time.

The Magic of Audio Taping

Boom boxes aren't glamorous but I love 'em. You may ask, "How is the boom box a neat tool that's going to up my efficiency?" The answer is that your typical boom box offers *tape-to-tape dubbing*—you can tape CDs or other tapes—and I don't just mean the fun stuff. I routinely tape meetings with key clients and associates, and then make copies for them. They appreciate it and it keeps everyone on the same footing. (Accuracy saves time!) Often I check out tapes and other audiovisual materials from the library but don't have time to play them before they're due back. By taping them, I can then play them at my leisure. When I get new materials, I often tape over the old ones so I'm not creating a huge collection. I can glean what I want to hear with no pressure to return the materials by a certain time.

Often, when I'm in a meeting with others, I use drive-time to review what transpired. While normally I don't champion doing two things at once, this can work well. Just don't attempt to take notes unless you pull off the road.

Go!
While traveling, if you want to review any cassettes or CDs you've dubbed, the portable players come in handy, particularly on airplanes. You can get an inexpensive earplug for private listening.

Having a portable cassette or CD player facilitates using a boom box. You can create the original recording with a portable recorder and then make a dub with the boom box.

I've used this setup to review my own speaking presentations, those of others, meetings, phone conversations, motivational tapes, and books-on-tape. I'll bet you can identify at least five opportunities in the next month that offer you benefits from recording an event and playing it back later.

The Least You Need to Know

➤ There will always be faster, sleeker, less expensive, more powerful gizmos to buy. Don't worry about it; get what works for you and learn to use it well.

➤ Each tool or technique to increase your efficiency carries the seeds of great benefits *and* significant drawbacks.

➤ You learn most technologies *when you need to*. There's no need to feel anxious or guilty if you don't possess "the state of the art" (though advertisers love it when you do).

➤ You need to adopt a piece of technology when your work requires it, your clients use it, or it offers a competitive advantage.

➤ Simple technologies such as tape-to-tape boom boxes, dictation equipment, and portable cassette players can also give you some control over your time. Don't overlook them.

Chapter 13

Handling Mail and Correspondence Quickly

In This Chapter

➤ Conventional ways to transfer information and messages will be around for a while

➤ Ways to save 60%–70% of your correspondence time

➤ Worthwhile options still brought to you by the good old Post Office

➤ Using a 31-day tickler file for timed responses

Mail moves the country, and ZIP codes move the mail—well, perhaps not anymore. Nevertheless, most messages you receive, whether in the form of e-mail, faxes, or memos, will require your response.

The faster and easier you are able to respond, the better your day, week, career, and life will be—and the more you'll be in control of your time.

There are many options available to you for speedily handling message replies.

What Do You Want to Send and Why?

If you're in sales (or another type of position where you initiate contact with potential customers), your mail and messages are *pro*active rather than *re*active. *You* initiate them to get another party interested in your goods or services, although it's likely that most of the information you send to others will be in response to requests they've made or an obligation you need to fulfill.

Handling Correspondence Quickly

Sometimes the correspondence you'd like to give a prompt response falls by the wayside; you have to care for too many other things. Here's a secret of winning back your time: When a response doesn't require formal business protocol (that is, when you know the other party well) or the item only merits brief regard, remember that there are many ways to handle it quickly—and use them. For example:

1. Some people use preprinted, plain-paper messages such as, "Excuse the informality, but I feel it's more important to respond promptly than to offer a more formal reply that would take much longer."

2. Retain the return address information on the envelopes from the mail you've received. Thereafter you can use the addresses as your address label back to them, and avoid having to engage your printer, copier, or label paper. Clip such addresses or tear them out with a ruler's edge.

   When I receive a package from someone, I clip the label from their package and attach it to the documents that came inside with a big paper clip or removable tape. When I'm ready to make a response, an address label to the other party is already available. (This will save you lots of time. When other people respond too slowly, often it's because they haven't devised a speedy reply system.)

Go!
Ask people how they feel when they receive such replies. Most prefer a quick, informal response that answers their question, rather than waiting weeks for a formal response that does the same.

3. Order a rubber stamper from your office supply store; it should say "Speed Reply." I have one myself; it's oversized and prints in bright red. When you receive a letter that merits a quick reply, stamp it with "Speed Reply" and offer your reply on the space at the bottom of the letter. Alternatively, you could print labels that say "Speed Reply" and simply affix them to the page.

   You have the option of faxing the letter (the fax machine treats deep, bold, red ink as black) or you could copy and mail the letter. Techniques like these enable you to get a reply to the other party quickly and give you a record of the correspondence. Such a response is helpful to recipients as well; it presents their message with your reply. Think of how many times you've written to someone, the person responded, and you couldn't remember why you wrote.

4. If you're mailing a response, insert one of your own address labels to help the other party keep in touch with you. I enclose my address label with nearly all correspondence I mail. If you surmise that you'll write the other party again, include extra address labels.

What a Concept!

Weeks afterward, you'll begin to notice happily that you receive replies more promptly—and the other party is using the address labels you provided. This tells you they've bought into your system.

When you've successfully trained your correspondents to communicate adeptly with you, both sides benefit.

5. Order a rubber stamp or create a label that facilitates your fax replies as well. It would include your name, phone, and fax number—offering your essential contact information. You would use it on any correspondence you receive; it avoids using up the recipient's fax paper.

Often, when you receive faxes from a free-standing fax machine, the other party uses a full page to announce that a fax is coming, and then uses another page for a six- or eight-line message. The whole communication could have taken one-third of a page. When you initiate a labeling system, you let other parties know you respect their time and resources—and you keep your costs down.

If you're using a fax/modem, the same principles apply. Keep your fax identification information concise and near the top of the first page. Keep your message brief; it makes a response likelier and keeps your transmission costs down.

6. For longer or more involved hard-copy correspondence, use the back side of the page you receive. Make a copy of the front and back for your own hard-copy files. Sometimes you can consolidate the correspondence you've received and do the same for what you send. For example, if someone sends you a two-page letter but you only need to respond to one key paragraph, simply clip that paragraph, include it at the top of your transmission, and reply below.

7. Feel free to number the points in the correspondence you've received and address each point in your reply. This cuts down on the time and energy it takes to reply. Otherwise you have to quote chapter and verse in your reply.

When you number the points in the correspondence you receive, you can usually address everything in a one-page response. Formal responses that take two or more pages require copy-editing and tedious tweaking. Worse, they suck time out of your day and life.

What a Concept!

While business and organizational protocol may often call for formal responses, your mission is to offer as many efficient, informal responses as you can.

8. Be on the lookout for creative ways to use your fax machine, fax/modem, printer, and copier in combination to generate fast, appropriate responses to messages you receive; don't let correspondence pile up.

9. Design forms to handle routine communication. Better yet, see if someone in your office has already created one, or assign that task to someone. Many office-supply stores carry books with predesigned correspondence forms. They're worth the $10 to $15; you're likely to save enough valuable time to pay for them the first day you use them.

Variations on Speed-Reply Options

You've probably figured this out, but it's worth mentioning: any time you want to respond to someone's message but you don't want a lengthy conversation, you can time your transmission to arrive when the person isn't in.

For example, if you're on the West Coast and it's 4:30 p.m., it's a safe bet that if you respond to someone on the East Coast by fax or voice mail, he or she won't be in at 7:30 p.m. to receive it. Your party will receive the fax the next day, which is fine with you, because you didn't want to talk to anyone anyway.

I frequently order office supplies by fax so I won't have to stay on the phone and spell things out to somebody who writes at a blinding snail's pace. I don't have to worry that the other party will record my information incorrectly. On a third or half of a page, with a fax/modem transmission, I can present everything I need to convey in seconds.

All About the Post Office: A Shattering Exposé

(Just kidding.) You already know about the express-mail services because you probably use them often—FedEx, UPS, and others. For all their troubles, it still makes sense to use the U. S. Postal Service—if you know how to use the system effectively. Here is a brief, alphabetical description from the public information at the postal service regarding their standard services. Following that is a description of services to safeguard, protect, and document your packages. Because the Postal Service is always changing their rates, I've left these out. You can call your local post office and with any luck you'll get somebody to give you the current rates.

Certified mail: This type provides you with a mailing receipt. A record of delivery is maintained at your receiver's Post Office. For valuables and irreplaceable items, the Postal Service recommends using insured or registered mail (they're coming up in this list).

Express Mail Next-Day service: This is the Post Office's fastest service. To use it, take your shipment to any designated Express Mail Post Office, generally by 5:00 p.m., or deposit it in an Express Mail collection box. Your package will be delivered to the addressee by 3:00 p.m. the next day (weekends and holidays included).

> **Warning**
> Too many professionals today indicate that they need more time to get their jobs done. Actually, that kind of thinking keeps you enslaved to the clock. More time is *not* on its way—and *it's not the solution* if you aren't operating efficiently.

First-class mail: It's designed for letters, postal cards, greeting cards, personal notes, and for sending checks and money orders. You cannot insure ordinary first-class mail.

Forwarding mail: When you move, fill out a "Change of Address" card in advance at your local post office. When possible, notify your post office at least one month before your move. First-class mail is forwarded at no charge. Magazines, newspapers, and other second-class mail are forwarded at no charge for 60 days.

Insurance: You can purchase it on registered mail, up to a maximum of $25,000, $500 for third- and fourth-class mail, and for merchandise mailed at the Priority Mail or first-class mail rates.

Priority mail: This is first-class mail (more than 12 ounces and up to 70 pounds, with size limitations) to be delivered within two business days. (Rumor has it that P.O. workers are P.O.'d about this category of mail.)

Registered mail: The Postal Service regards this as their most secure mailing option. Postal insurance may be purchased (up to a maximum of $25,000); return receipts and restricted delivery services are available for an additional fee.

Restricted delivery: Restricted delivery means that delivery is made only to the addressee or to someone who is authorized in writing to receive mail for the addressee.

Return receipt: This is your proof of delivery; it's available on mail that you send by COD or Express Mail, mail insured for more than $25, or that you registered or certified. The return receipt shows who signed for the item and the date it was delivered.

Special delivery: You can buy special-delivery service on all classes of mail except bulk third-class. Delivery happens even on Sundays and holidays, during hours that extend beyond the hours for delivery of ordinary mail.

Tickler Files for Timed Responses

In Chapter 11, I discussed setting up a file for each month, and a 31-day rotating tickler file. These files offered a home for things that you didn't need to deal with immediately, or that were best dealt with at some future time. To handle mail quickly, tickler files are just what the time-saving doctor ordered.

Suppose you receive correspondence that doesn't have to be answered now. What are you going to do? Let it sit in your in-basket? Park it some place on your desk? Create some new file for it? All these temporary solutions are less than desirable.

While it may make sense to handle the correspondence now if it needn't be transmitted till later, do what you have to do with it and then park it in your tickler file. For example, if you receive something on the 5th that need not be mailed until the 15th (to reach the other party by the 19th), take care of it today while it's hot, fresh, and right in front of you. Seal it, stamp it, and put it in your tickler file for the 15th.

Go!
Anytime you have hard-copy correspondence you need to attend to, but it's best sent at another time, the tickler file is your answer.

The electronic version of this technique is to type your e-mail message and then enter the date and time you want it submitted.

You may recall that a tickler file is an ideal way to stay on top of bills without paying them too early (which can cost you if you have an interest-bearing checking account) and avoiding penalties for paying too late.

Here are some other ways to use your tickler file for timed responses that save your time and help put you on top of things:

➤ Stash tickets to forthcoming events in the appropriate tickler-file date.

➤ Store coupons, discounts, and promotional items until you're ready to use them.

➤ Park items you want to read on your next plane trip in the tickler file for the day before your trip.

➤ Find temporary locations for notes, outlines, or other documents you'll want to have on hand when someone visits your office.

➤ Do the same for forthcoming group, department, or company meetings.

➤ Place any mail you receive *but choose not to open now* in your tickler file; choose a date that seems more appropriate for you.

➤ When you're waiting for someone's response, file a copy of your transmission in your tickler file or in a file labeled "Awaiting Response."

The Least You Need to Know

➤ Put down this book and order a long-life stamper from an office supply store (it should say "speed reply") or create labels using your PC and printer. Start using your speed-reply message on correspondence right away.

➤ Check out submitting legal contracts via the fax. You can also become adept at negotiating via fax.

➤ Depending on what you want to send, and to whom, the U.S. Postal System (for all its shortcomings) has a variety of services that may provide what you need.

➤ Set up a 31-day, rotating tickler file system so that when you have correspondence to handle but prefer to send it later, you have a convenient place to park it.

Part 3
Thinking Your Way Around Time Traps

Consider what you've been up to in the first two parts of the book: leaving the office on time, choosing priorities, getting help, and recognizing that we are all in the same boat. Then you went in quest of getting more sleep, not being overwhelmed by tasks and information, whipping your office and files into shape, and using tools profitably. Maybe none of the individual changes were too huge, but you've been busy. By contrast, you're going to like the next three chapters—the tips and recommendations require less work! You can simply think your way through some situations, and they'll come out all right!

In Chapter 14, "Making Big Decisions in Record Time," you'll see why you're facing way too many decisions in a day, and that the more decisions you have to make, the harder it gets to make any. In Chapter 15, "One Thing at a Time," you'll discover a fundamental secret (oops! the title gives it away) on how to slow down the clock once and for all. In Chapter 16, "The Urge to Merge and Purge," you'll learn how to be on the lookout for the bells and whistles that overcomplicate your life. Complexity is a tricky character. There you are, minding your own business, and before you know it, BOOM! Complications land on you like a ton of individual bricks. You didn't even realize you were aiding and abetting the dumping. Once complications take hold, they spread like kudzu in Tennessee; beating them back becomes increasingly difficult.

To begin, here's a look at making big decisions in record time, and making small decisions not at all.

Chapter 14

Making Big Decisions in Record Time

In This Chapter

➤ The growing number of choices, hence decisions, you'll face

➤ When it's best to avoid making a decision

➤ How more data can confound your ability to decide

➤ Using the power of your intuitive capabilities

Decisions, decisions. Some are big; most are trivial. Any way you look at it, you're confronted by too many decisions—at work, at home, on the weekend, while traveling, when you wake, when you retire at night, when you're on vacation, and when you're with either friends or enemies.

Why are you facing more decisions? Is it because you're getting older and have more responsibilities? Is it because you have a bigger bank account (ha-ha)? Or is something else bringing on the change? As you may remember, Chapter 3 discussed how anyone holding a responsible job may feel time-pressed; *everyone's in the same boat.*

More Choices Mean More Decisions

In a world of six billion people and counting, more information is being generated—and sped your way by worldwide media and print coverage.

It's not hard to understand why you face too much information. Society spews it in abundance. For example, the White House is covered by *1,800* reporters! (You'd think maybe three or four hundred could do the job....) When the media cover something they can sink their teeth into, they sink them deep.

When you go to the drug store to buy something as inconsequential as shampoo or skin care lotion, watch out. There are more than 1,200 varieties of shampoo on the market, and more than 2,000 skin-care products. Choices abound in other arenas. More than 6,000 popular videos are available for viewing (more than 64,000 if you include management training, aerobic fitness, and how-tos). Three thousand books are published in the U.S.A. each week—more than 600 a day. Ten times as many radio stations exist today than when television was first introduced. If these examples don't indicate an example of "choice overload," I don't know what will.

In his landmark book, *Future Shock*, Alvin Toffler said that in the future too many choices would be competing for your time and attention. In a word, he was right. Manufacturers engage in *mass-customization* to offer you products with whatever bells and whistles you want (and ads make you want them). When Lee Iacocca was the chief executive officer of Chrysler, he converted all the company's car dealers to the concept of mass-customization. The customer comes in, orders a basic car, and then adds the specifics—tinted glass, whitewalls, automatic steering or power brakes, among several dozen options.

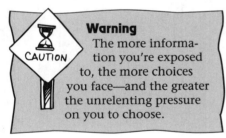

Warning
The more information you're exposed to, the more choices you face—and the greater the unrelenting pressure on you to choose.

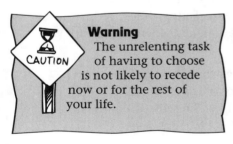

Warning
The unrelenting task of having to choose is not likely to recede now or for the rest of your life.

Theoretically, with the perfect information, after having whittled down your search to the essence of your needs, you could purchase any product you seek. There's only one problem—you hardly ever get to have even *semi*-perfect information (at least in this life). So you're forever besieged by too much information—much of it conflicting—and it impedes your ability to choose. To win back more of your time, identify the big decisions and make them quickly. Start by determining which decisions are *worth making*, and which are worth forsaking.

Decisions Worth Making

Think back to Chapters 5 and 6; review the discussion on establishing priorities and goals. What you establish as important in your life is immediately linked to decisions that are *worth making.*

When something will have a significant impact in the area of one of your life's priorities, there's a decision worth making. Anything less than that is a decision worth forsaking—but I'm getting ahead of myself. Many people mix decisions worth making with those worth forsaking, treat them almost equally, and wonder where the time went.

If your boss requested that you make a decision, the situation is clear-cut. Nevertheless, decisions worth making are often conditional. If you're single and trying to choose between two likely mates, your decision *will* affect the quality of your life in the foreseeable future—and perhaps the rest of your life. The following are examples of decisions worth making:

➤ The choice of a spouse.

➤ The choice of a home.

➤ Major work decisions your organization requests of you.

➤ Where you'll live.

➤ With whom you'll associate.

➤ What course of study you'll pursue.

➤ Whether you wish to climb to the top of your organization or profession.

Decisions worth making, while often conditional, are not always apparent. Consider the following five issues. Are they decisions worth spending any time on? It all depends. In the list that follows, mentally circle the decisions you believe worth making:

➤ The color of the next toothbrush you buy.

➤ The next movie you see.

➤ Whether to attend the next PTA meeting.

➤ Whether to take your car in for a tune-up tomorrow.

➤ What to eat for breakfast.

Have you finished circling the items above? Good. So what are the right answers? As you may have guessed, there are none.

1. **The color of the next toothbrush.** For most people this is a decision worth forsaking; it can't be that important. When might it be? If the decor of your home and bathroom is of utmost importance to you (don't laugh, it is for some people) then this becomes a decision worth making.

2. **The next movie you see.** It's likely you only go to movies you think you'll enjoy; when you see one you didn't like, it was a mistake, but the earth didn't tremble. If you consider movies as just a way to pass the time, then which one you see is not of paramount or universal importance.

   When would it be? If improving the cultural component of your life is among your priorities, and the movie is of the shoot-'em-up variety, your decision is clear: Don't go see it. Of the hundreds of movies you've seen in your life, how many have truly had a significant impact on your behavior and activities? Few, if any. Granted, seeing *Schindler's List* may heighten your sensitivity to vital historical issues. More often than not, however, choosing a movie is no big deal.

3. **Going to the next PTA meeting.** If your child's education or the betterment of your community is a high priority, you would attend. If your child is doing extremely well in school or you're pleased about the school system in general, you could skip one meeting, or a run of them. If it's a toss-up between going to the PTA meeting or seeing a movie, your priorities are pretty clear.

4. **Should you put your car in the shop tomorrow?** Has your car been running poorly lately? What is the cost of you being tied up on the highway and not getting into work on time, and causing 10,000 people to snarl at you? Can you bring work with you to the repair shop, or can they give you a ride back to work quickly after your arrival? Is preventive maintenance part of your overall plan to be ready and stay on top of things?

Go!
If 29 times out of 30 you eat a healthy breakfast and *one* day you decide to splurge on high-cholesterol, high-fat, and highly sugared items, you're not likely to upset the benefits of good breakfast habits.

5. **What to eat for breakfast.** If you're already 32 pounds above your ideal and have no hope of ever getting back into shape, what you eat for breakfast tomorrow morning matters less than the longer-term health concerns you're facing—go ahead and have that (*one*) honey-glazed doughnut with your coffee. If becoming the first octogenarian to visit the moon is a priority for you, then the choice is clear: go healthy instead.

Decisions Worth Forsaking

Decisions worth forsaking are always lying around. They ought to be easy to spot, but when you're faced with too many decisions anyway, your reflex action likely to be an attempt to take on all decisions.

What's a *low-level decision*? When a coworker asks you where you want to go to lunch today, your response will most appropriately be, "You decide." Of the couple thousand times you've been to lunch, can you recall any significant impact related to your decision on where you went? Okay, so one day you met somebody you started dating. Another time, you learned something new. In general, there hasn't been much impact. Other examples of decisions worth forsaking include:

Warning
As a general principle, avoid making all low-level decisions.

➤ The park or playground where you'll take your children to play; let them decide.

➤ Whether to catch the news at ten or not.

➤ Whether to get Del Monte frozen vegetables or Bird's Eye frozen vegetables.

➤ Whether to visit Colorado for five days or six.

You may be asking if there is any perceptible benefit to making fewer choices per day. To answer this question, I offer the following anecdote. The Los Angeles Lakers, under Coach Pat Riley, would fly on chartered planes following their games; the players never had to wait. Each player had the same seat on every plane, bus, and cab. Magic Johnson said (in his autobiography *My Life)* that although this was a small thing, the players found it comforting and reassuring. Kareem Abdul Jabbar always sat across from James Worthy. Magic Johnson and Michael Cooper always sat behind Kareem. Magic said that after a long, hard game, he would jump on the bus or plane and know exactly where to sit. Riley took this low-level choice out of the hands of the players.

Consider an instance of good manners in this light. When you go to a dinner party and the host has already assigned seating to the guests, it's an act of kindness. It reduces anxiety about who'll be in the chair beside you. This is a time-honored tradition from Walnut Creek, California, to the White House.

Avoiding the Paralysis of Analysis

If you find yourself overanalyzing situations too frequently, *relent*. You're a product of Western civilization; you've been trained from birth to collect all the data, statistics, articles, reports, and information you could lay hands on before making a decision that involves the outlay of any sizeable sum.

When each individual in two groups of executives had to make a large purchase decision for their respective companies, the first group was armed with information—reports, data, statistics, and all that jazz. Understandably, each one used *all the information* to make the purchase decision.

The second group consisted of individuals who had no such data or statistics. They used instinct, or intuition, or whatever you want to call it. Weeks after the purchases had been made and each executive got to see the results, which group do you expect was happier with their decisions? (Well, okay, I *did* load the question a little to favor the second group.)

Honestly, though, you would be likelier to have chosen the group that had the data and statistics. Moreover, if given a chance to be in one group or the other, you would have chosen to be *in* that well-informed group, wouldn't you? How could the second group *possibly* be happier? If you're 30 or 40 or 50 years old, everything you've learned in your life up to now is brought to bear when you make a decision. There's far more to instinct or intuition than is generally acknowledged.

Warning
Paradoxically, more data is not always the answer; sometimes it can impede your progress.

Warning
Much of the data you collect may be redundant, reaffirming what you already know. Too often, you may unconsciously be *collecting* what you already know or believe, without seeing the data objectively.

There are also inherent traps in collecting more data on the way to making a decision. For example, the more data you collect, *the likelier it is you'll get conflicting answers*.

Sometimes the data that you collect is nothing more than a crutch. Or its only purpose is to cover your derrière (if the decision turns out unfavorable), by having an authority to cite: "It says right here blah, blah, blah."

Sometimes the data you collect is a substitute for taking action. Studying a decision is a classic way to delay making it. (The government has done it for years.) In all cases, whatever data or information you collect has to be *applied*.

More data is not always the answer, but what's the alternative? I'll deal with intuition in a moment. For now, here are some techniques for making big decisions in record time, getting the answer you want with less effort:

1. **Three calls away from any expert.** If you could identify the single best person to call to start off your information search, you can get your answer within two more calls. Who's the first person to call? It could be your municipal or college library, an official of an industry or professional association, or an information service firm (such as market researchers). Perhaps you can find an expert within government, or an editor at *Consumer Reports*.

2. **Finding the trailblazer.** Has anyone else already made a decision like this? If so, and their circumstances are somewhat similar to yours, it would behoove you to learn what they discovered. It pays to network with people in your field. Later you can tap them for their experiences (abbreviated with the technical term O.P.E.— other people's experiences).

3. **Consensus building.** Can you assemble a group, hash it out, and base your decision on the consensus reached? In many instances this will work fine. After all, you relied on the power of the group; if your decision crashes and burns, you can always point the finger at them (just kidding!).

4. **The answer will simply emerge.** This alleviates a lot of decisions. It's like the U.S. pulling out of Somalia; often, as circumstances unfold, the decision that makes the most sense becomes apparent. If you suspect this might be the case, sit back and let time takes its course. The answer may become abundantly clear.

Decisions in the Form of Problems

Quite a few decisions you have to make are based on problems. Modern management theory holds that problems can be approached productively when you see them as opportunities or challenges. Robert Fritz, in *The Path of Least Resistance*, suggests that you view problems as your best friends. It often works!

How does facing a problem help you to get to higher ground? This view of problem solving works best when you're not dealing with extremes—the death of a loved one or (on the other hand) a hangnail. If the decision you face is a disguised problem, try treating it as your best friend or a teacher with wisdom to impart. You may dislodge something in your decision-making process and proceed more easily.

Biographers have noted that Ben Franklin, when faced with big decisions, listed the pluses and minuses of one path versus another. Sometimes he gave weight to them; sometimes he didn't. While this is a basic approach to making decisions, listing your potential options on paper still beats merely weighing them in your mind; you can keep better track of them this way.

I find it's best to strive for solutions that encompass both short-term and long-term remedies. If you put a bandage on an eight-inch gash, it might hold temporarily, but you could end up with gangrene.

Go!
If you come up with a decision that both addresses the immediate situation and provides long-term benefits, then you've got something.

In *Feel the Fear and Do It Anyway*, Dr. Susan Jeffers suggests that when you encounter a decision to be made that represents a hurdle or a roadblock, you need to let yourself feel all the emotions that arise. Are you uneasy? Quivering? Lightheaded? Is your stomach upset, are you trembling, or do you feel fearful? Once you're honest with yourself about how you feel, initiate your decision anyway, Jeffers says. Often you're able to break through your fear and overcome the obstacle that loomed so large when you weren't being honest with yourself. (Hmm, sounds like it's worth a try.)

Speed Decision-Making

Interested in the *fastest* way to make decisions? This involves using your instincts or intuition. You're already pretty good at this; you got this far in life and, hey, it ain't so bad. Write down your intuitive choice before making any final decision. Then, when enough time has passed to see some results of a more analytical decision, write them down and compare them to the results of your intuitive choice. As time passes, you'll begin to notice how frequently your intuitive choices were good ones, and find yourself trusting your hunches more easily and more often.

What a Concept!

Once you get adept at trusting your intuition, you can bypass many realms of data and information that previously impeded your ability to choose. You can call upon your still, quiet, faithful, internal guidance system.

Intuition in Action

Do you have a dentist? It's a reasonable question. How did you select your dentist? Did you open up the phone book and get the names of the ten to twelve dentists nearest you, then call each of them, decide (based on the call) to visit five to seven, visit their offices, grill each one on billing procedures, background, expertise, competency of their staff, office hours, prices, and overall philosophy? Then did you whittle down the list to maybe two or three, call them back or visit on another occasion, do some background checking for reputation, longevity in the community, and professional standing? Then, and only then, did you decide on dentist A? Or did you choose dentist B on the basis of who your parents or friends see, where some referral service sent you, or simply the clever ad you saw in the phone book?

You probably used the latter method, picking a dentist by hook or by crook—and if that one didn't work out, you switched. In short, you used a *combination* of references and intuitive processes to come up with your dentist.

Why, then, do you overcomplicate so many decisions at work and in the rest of your life? When you base a choice on intuition, every cell in your body and every shred of intelligence you've ever accumulated are brought to bear. There's a lot going on behind the solutions you make.

What a Concept

Pay attention to your small voice; it's there to support you if you listen to it.

New information is only going to hit you faster and faster as your life proceeds. You'll be able to absorb and use only a fraction of what you're exposed to. There's no time for exhaustive research on every consumer product you buy (ever try counting how many different ones you use?). You're going to have to trust your instincts.

Suppose, on the other hand, you're considering whether to move to town A or town B. What factors would you logically consider? Try these out:

➤ Housing prices

➤ Taxes, demographics

➤ Schools

➤ Crime

➤ Community groups

➤ Family and friends

➤ Lakes, streams, and beaches

➤ Trails and mountains

➤ The business community

➤ Population density

➤ Education levels

➤ Nearby colleges

➤ Churches, synagogues, mosques

➤ Road systems

➤ Major highway access

➤ Shopping

➤ Traffic patterns

➤ Deviant groups

You guessed it—there are dozens of factors you could analyze and compare. In the end, your decision would probably be based on some combination of data (though not too much) and intuition (probably a lot).

Blasting Through Procrastination

When faced with too many decisions, your natural inclination may be to procrastinate—or perhaps you fear making a mistake. Don't beat yourself up (that can be a way to delay action further); lots of people face this problem. Decisions that would normally roll off your back become more involved when there's too much on your plate—and chances are, there's too much on your plate. Here's a list of ways to break through the procrastination that stymies your decision-making:

➤ **Face procrastination head-on.** What is blocking you, what is the real reason you don't want to choose? Write it down or record it on cassette. This exercise alone may dislodge something and help you decide.

➤ **Choose to easily begin.** Make a positive affirmation of yourself: "I can easily make this decision." This affirmation has power and is often enough. Elizabeth Jeffries, a Louisville, Kentucky-based speaker and trainer for health-care organizations, maintains a list of daily affirmations that help her make decisions she could otherwise put off.

➤ **Find the easy point.** Ask yourself, "What are three to five things I could do to progress toward the final decision, *without* actually tackling it head-on?" Then initiate these "easy entry" activities. Often they're enough to get you fully involved.

➤ **Set up your desk for a decision.** Set up your desk or office to enable you to focus on the decision at hand; ignore other (less important) matters. This might involve neatly arranging papers, file folders, reports, and other items. Working at a clear desk leaves only the issue at hand in front of you.

Probably 95 percent of your decisions will have only a minimal impact on your life; don't let the fear of being wrong shackle you unduly.

Making Purchase Decisions

When you need to make a purchase decision, sometimes all you need is a good set of questions to ask. Without further ado, here's a checklist of questions for making sound purchase decisions more quickly:

❏ Are there quantity discounts, economic ordering quantities, or special terms?

❏ Are there corporate, government, association, military, or educators' discounts?

❏ Do they give weekly, monthly, quarterly seasonal discounts?

❏ Do they give off-peak discounts, odd-lot discounts?

❏ Do they offer a guaranteed lowest price?

❏ Do they accept major credit cards?

❏ Do they accept orders by fax? e-mail?

❏ Do they offer a money-back guarantee, or other guarantee?

❏ Do they have an 800 ordering fax line or toll-free customer service line?

❏ Do they guarantee the shipping date? How do they ship?

❏ Do they offer free delivery? Free installation?

❏ Will they keep your name off their mailing list (unless you want to keep up with special sales)?

❏ Do they intend to sell, rent, or otherwise transfer your name and ordering information to others?

❏ Are their shipments insured?

❏ Are there shipping and handling charges? Are their prices guaranteed? Is there tax?

❏ Are there any other charges?

❏ Do they have free samples?

❏ Are authorized dealer/repair services in your area?

❏ Are references or referral letters available?

❏ Are there satisfied customers in your area?

❏ How long have they been in business?

❏ Who are they owned by?

❏ How long for delivery?

❏ Is gift-wrapping available?

❏ Does the product come with a warranty?

The Least You Need to Know

➤ From now till the end of your life you're likely to face *more* decisions per day or week—not fewer. Get in the habit of focusing on decisions that advance your priorities and support your goals.

➤ Avoid making low-level decisions whenever possible.

➤ Remember that more data is not always the answer. Trust your instincts more often; they are there to serve you.

➤ If the decision represents a problem, consider seeing it as a friend and messenger. With that perspective, ask what the problem is helping you to do or overcome.

➤ Using a prepared checklist can greatly enhance a purchasing decision. Feel free to copy the one given here.

Chapter 15

One Thing at a Time

In This Chapter

➤ The fallacy of doing several things at once to "save" time

➤ Tips on practicing doing one thing at a time

➤ Devising an interruption-management system

I'm willing to bet the farm that sometime in the last 48 hours, if not the last four hours, you engaged in some form of *multitasking*—doing two or more things at the same time. It's likely you've been working on a personal computer recently, and that while you were running the word-processing software, you may have been engaging the printer, a pop-up spreadsheet, and a calendar as well.

Computers—from the notebook PC that sits on your lap while you fly to the huge Cray supercomputers that fill rooms—are well equipped to handle more than one task at a time; *human beings, however, are not computers*, no matter what you may have heard. Stay tuned; this chapter will explore this case of mistaken identity.

The Misfortune of Multitasking

When you are working with your PC, trying to answer the phone or open mail, trying to respond to the fax machine or the request from the next head to pop in your door—and whatever else you can add to this list, and you attempt to entertain them all—you are attempting to engage in multitasking. It's a computer term; there's a reason for that—it's a computer function. Unlike the computer, you're likely to do an unsatisfactory job when you multitask.

Why One Thing?

All things considered, you work best when you focus on one thing at a time. On many levels you probably know this already, but when is the last time you practiced it? Probably not recently. It's too easy to fall into a familiar trap: "So much is expected of me, I have to double and triple my activities."

Warning
At the workplace and at home, trying to multitask ensures that you'll miss your day, week, and ultimately your life. I know people who are 40 years old who can't remember where their thirties went, and people who are 50 who can't remember where their forties went.

Nearly every message in society says it's okay—or necessary—to double or triple the number of activities you perform at once. You see advertisements of people talking on the phone while they watch television, or eating while they read.

Bob W., age 41, works for a large brokerage firm in the International Square building in Washington. He is friendly, successful, and always in a rush. He talks fast, moves fast, eats fast, and never lets up. Bob is hooked on multitasking. Many executive and career climbers suffer from a misdirected sense of urgency stemming from far too many tasks and responsibilities. Certainly, it's appropriate to work more quickly than normal at certain times. It's a problem when it becomes a standard operating procedure.

The Decade of the Brain

In 1990 the House Committee on Appropriations asked the Department of Health and Human Services, the National Advisory of Neurological Disorders and Stroke Council, and the National Advisory of Mental Health Council to prepare a report for Congress on how scientists working through the federal government could have a unique opportunity to advance and apply scientific knowledge about the brain and the nervous system. (Ah, for once, a new complaint—"tax dollars down the brain.")

The published report ("The Decade of the Brain") stated that researchers have learned more about the brain and nervous system during the last ten years than throughout all of history—and progress during the next decade promises to be spectacular.

"What is so remarkable is that the brain both coordinates major bodily functions and provides the capacity for self-awareness, for learning, and for adapting to an ever-changing environment," the report says. "The development of this marvelous machine is dependent upon processes that are set into motion at conception and result in a structure consisting of billions of cells."

Too Much Brain Power?

Superior intelligence has enabled human beings to dominate the planet, while simultaneously holding the potential for human extinction. In *The Run Away Brain: The Evolution of Human Uniqueness*, author Christopher Wills observes that human brainpower has enabled the species to multiply in unreasonable numbers, putting such pressure on the planet that ecological and nuclear catastrophes have become a real possibility.

Wills argues that "surely we are now too smart to go on breeding ourselves to extinction, destroying most of the rest of the species on the planet in the process. Surely we are too smart to blow ourselves up with nuclear weapons invented by our runaway brains." (We can hope....)

When you do two things at once, it's probably symptomatic of an ability (and burden) shared by the whole human species. That doesn't necessarily make it effective. The false economy of attempting to do two things at once is ingrained in a culture that rewards the workaholic, the 16-hour-a-day entrepreneur, the supermom, and the hyper-energetic high-school student.

What's more, the mental and psychic toll you place on yourself in attempting multitasking (or in doing one stressful job for too long) can be harmful. Your brain can become overtaxed!

Consider the case of air-traffic controllers who have been on duty too long, had too many planes come in at a given time, and have the responsibility of keeping hundreds of lives safe by making the right decisions with split-second timing. It's no wonder that this is a high-stress, high-burnout position, one that professionals usually abandon at a young age.

Warning
Any time you undertake original or creative thinking—work with numbers, charts, or graphs, write, copy-edit, or proofread—diverting your attention is bound to result in far less than your best effort; often it leads to costly errors.

When Do You Work Best?

Researchers at the Medical College of Wisconsin have found that if you perform as simple a task as tapping your foot, you activate the primary motor in your cortex, a section of

Etched in Stone

"Men give me some credit for genius. All the genius I have lies in this: When I have a subject at hand I study it profoundly. Day and night it is before me. I explore it in all its bearings. My mind becomes pervaded with it. Then the effort which I have made is what people are pleased to call the fruit of genius. It is instead the fruit of labor and thought." —Alexander Hamilton

your brain. If your task is more involved, if it includes planning in order to tap your foot to a sequence (such as one-two, one-two-three, one-two, one-two-three), then *two* secondary motor areas in the front of the cortex are engaged. You are drawing upon more of your brain's functioning capacity.

Don't worry, your brain can handle it. The point is that when you engage in multitasking—such as attempting to watch TV while eating, or doodling while you talk on the telephone—your brain functioning changes to incorporate the extra activities.

If you want to do the best at whatever you're doing, allow your brain to concentrate on one activity—focus on one thing at a time. If it's a complex task, consider whether you're working on several parts of the *same* task or *two different tasks*. It sounds simple enough, but this advice goes against the grain of a society that tells you to do many things at once so you can "be more efficient." You see this every day: someone jogging down the road listening to a Walkman, doing work or reading while eating lunch. People double their activities, as if that will make things easier and better.

I sometimes do a little exercise with my audiences when speaking at conventions and executive retreats. I ask audience members to take out their watches and do nothing but stare at them for a solid minute. No one can do it! In this society, you're fed a message that emphasizes the importance of motion and activity. Merely reading, thinking, or reflecting doesn't *look busy enough*.

Has the following happened to you? Somebody walks by your desk and, horror of horrors, you're reading! Maybe the person looks at you a little funny, or perhaps you feel a bit guilty because you're not "in motion." Yet studies show that informed people in executive positions need to read professional journals and reports for two to four hours each day. So to be as productive as you need to be, you often act in ways that run *counter* to what society tells you is "productive activity."

To reach your full potential, you've got to break out of the mind-set imposed by others. Sometimes the best way to be productive is to sit at your desk doing *nothing*—at least nothing that looks like anything to people walking by. Reading or looking out the window in contemplation could be the single most important and productive thing you do in a day. Too often, you probably throw your time at tasks when you really need to reflect on them first.

What happens when you jump between different projects? It may feel "dynamic"—after all, you're exerting lots of energy. Yet there's a loss of productivity. You and a friend can test this easily at your desk or table. Decide on any three minor tasks in which the two of you can engage simultaneously. One task could be stacking pennies; another could be drawing 15 stars on a blank sheet of paper; a third could be linking paper clips. You each have the same number of items.

Go!
The single best way to cope with a number of different projects is to begin working on one thing until its completion, and then go on to the next project, and then the next, until you are finished.

You and your friend start these tasks at the same time. You stack a few pennies at a time, make a few stars on a blank piece of paper, and link some paper clips, indiscriminately alternating between the three tasks. Meanwhile, on the other side of the table, your friend stacks an equal number of pennies to completion—until there are no more. Then (s)he turns to making stars on a page, and reaches 15. Finally comes linking the paper clips till they're all linked.

Who do you think will not only finish faster and easier, but be in better shape mentally and emotionally? I'll bet on your friend *who focused on the task at hand, took it to completion, then turned to the next one* while you (ha-ha-ha) were bouncing back and forth between activities. You may have been more prone to errors, such as knocking over one of your stacks of pennies. Even if you were quite an adept task-juggler, you simply couldn't keep pace. The quality of your work was not as good. Perhaps your paper folds were not precise, or the 15 stars you drew on the page lacked a little artistic merit.

Multiply the effect of this simple test by the number of times you flip-flop between activities *in a day or year*, and it's easy to understand why you're not getting the best of all that activity. Continually switching from task to task is just not as productive as staying on one job until completion.

Give Yourself a Break

For today, give yourself the benefit of working on one thing at a time. You may have to switch gears when the boss comes in, when that important phone call comes through, or if you receive a fax that has to be acted on right away. When you switch gears, switch them entirely: give your complete and undivided attention to the pressing issue at hand. Try it out. You might agree that this is a happier, more effective way to work.

If you notice yourself falling into behavior patterns that resemble a computer multitasking, try these solutions:

➤ Take a 15-minute break once during the morning and once in the afternoon. That also means: Don't eat at your desk. Get away so you can recharge your battery.

➤ Invest in equipment or technology that offers you a significant return, that is, it pays for itself within one year or less, or saves at least two hours a week of your time.

➤ Hold regular meetings with your team to discuss how everyone can be more efficient—without multitasking. Focus on the big picture of what you're all trying to accomplish. Often, new solutions to old problems will emerge and activities that seem urgent can be viewed from a broader prospective.

➤ For a more human workplace, furnish your office with plants, pictures, art, or decorations that inspire creativity.

Remember Who Created the Situation

Robert Fritz (cited in Chapter 14) says that when you are feeling overwhelmed or time-stressed, ask yourself, "Who created this situation?" The answer is usually *you*.

Of course, there are times when the boss lays a bombshell on your desk and you're asked to do more than usual. It's still your responsibility to head off this threat to your time. You need to invest in resources that will equip you to handle tasks that come your way—whether it's new software, learning a new language, or acquiring more training.

Interruption Management

A few years ago, author Alvin Toffler told me that the workplace is a *terrible* place to get things done these days. With the distractions in your office, it's often better to work at the library, in the conference room, or on a park bench. This is especially true when you're doing conceptual or breakthrough thinking—when you need to have quiet space.

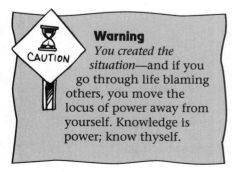

Warning
You created the situation—and if you go through life blaming others, you move the locus of power away from yourself. Knowledge is power; know thyself.

I was once consulting for a supervisor in Minnesota with six employees; he wanted to use his time more efficiently. He said his employees came to him with questions every couple of hours. That seemed harmless enough, but look at how it built up: If an employee asked a question every two hours, the supervisor got four from that person each day.

With six employees, that meant 24 questions a day, or 120 interruptions each week, resulting in disruptions of the manager's work three times each hour in a 40-hour week! I devised a system to help him cope with the interruptions and gain control of his time and called it the "J-4 System." (The *J* was for Jeff. You can use your own initial.)

I had the supervisor put the questions into four categories of manageability. The first distraction, J-1, was already answered in print and did not need a personal reply (it was in the company policy manual). The supervisor was then able to tell his employees, "Please don't bother me with J-1 distractions."

The second distraction, J-2, was a question that a peer or bookkeeper could answer; the supervisor did not need to be bothered with this type of question.

J-3s needed only a straightforward, short answer of yes or no. Such questions required interaction with the supervisor, but not much—a quick phone call or buzz on the intercom.

The final category, J-4 distractions, *required* the supervisor's input—he had to, and desired to, answer them.

How many questions were at the J-4 level of importance? Even assuming each person asked two J-4 questions per day—60 interruptions each week—this would cut the number of interruptions in half! Almost immediately, the supervisor was able to better use his time and reduce his level of stress.

As you do, you'll gain greater control over your work, you'll find more time, and feel more relaxed as that knot in your stomach begins to unravel. You'll even be able to do breakthrough creative thinking at your own desk.

Go!
Classify the types of interruptions you receive; then you can cut them down and cope with them better.

The number of distractions—the things competing for your time and attention—is infinite. You're only going to have more distractions in the future, not fewer. To regain control over your life, learn to cope with distractions in new ways.

The Pull of Anxiety

I once heard anxiety defined as *the attempted unification of opposing forces*. What majesty—this says it all. Anytime you're anxious, stop and figure out what opposing forces you're attempting to unite. Are you working on some low-level task when there's something far more important for you to give your attention to? You feel anxious. Your intuitive alarm is ringing.

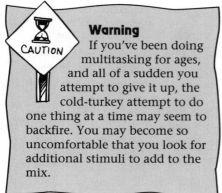

Warning
If you've been doing multitasking for ages, and all of a sudden you attempt to give it up, the cold-turkey attempt to do one thing at a time may seem to backfire. You may become so uncomfortable that you look for additional stimuli to add to the mix.

Your anxiety stems from your attempt to work on a low-level project (force #1) when you know there's something else that's more appropriate for you to be working on (force #2).

If you've been multitasking for a long time, and suddenly attempt to switch to working on one thing at a time, guess what happens? You may feel anxiety related to working on one thing at a time. It's like trying to kick an addiction to a chemical stimulant. You want to get off, and know you'll be better for doing it. But as you attempt to do without the stimulant, maybe you don't feel so good. The natural inclination is to get back into the addiction. So it is with multitasking—*what if that "dynamic" feeling is no more than an unproductive high?*

Exercises to Get in the Habit of One-Thing-at-a-Time

To become a master of doing one thing at a time, pick an activity you enjoy, where there's a high probability that you can engage in it without doing anything else. It might be driving your car with the radio off, reading in your favorite armchair without having any munchies, or just *listening* to music instead of banishing it to the background.

➤ Start with small segments. If you're reading in your favorite armchair, promise yourself you'll go ten minutes without any munchies the first night. The second night, go 15—then 20, and so forth. Eventually you may get to the point where you can read for an hour or more without having to resort to munchies.

➤ If you're trying to read, engage in conceptual or breakthrough thinking, or do some creative problem-solving, find as quiet and comfortable a place as possible.

➤ If you're surrounded by all manner of tasks competing for your attention, identify the one that's most important to tackle and stay with it until completion (or for as long as you can). If you're temporarily pulled away by something else, return to the important task at hand; again, stay with it to completion or for as long as you can.

➤ If you are paid to handle a multiplicity of items competing for your attention, practice giving short bursts of *full attention* to the task at hand, before turning to the next thing demanding your attention.

Consider an airline reservation attendant in the middle of a pressure situation. The approach is *one person and ticket situation at a time*; often the attendant doesn't even look up from the computer monitor. The same principle holds for a good bank teller, a good bus driver, or a construction worker walking on scaffolding five stories above the ground.

➤ Initiate personal balancing techniques: take deep breaths, stare out the window, see yourself as tackling the situation easily. Or try closing your eyes for a few seconds before confronting the task again. (More on this in Chapters 17 and 18.)

➤ Observe the people in your organization who concentrate well. What do they do that's different from what everybody else does? Talk to them; learn from them.

➤ If it's necessary, bring earplugs to work. Use a sound screen if it helps. (See Chapter 8.)

➤ Let others in on your quest to increase your powers of concentration. Mutual reinforcement can help.

➤ Practice using the interruption-management system discussed earlier in this chapter.

When It's Okay to Double Up Activities

For the most part, leave the multitasking to the computers. There are a few times when it's perfectly permissible to do more than one thing at a time—*and most of these occur away from work*. Obviously, at dinner with a friend or loved one you'll be talking and eating simultaneously—*but that can be seen as one event* (in some parts of the South, they call it "visiting" and it claims a person's whole attention). Generally, it's okay to drive and listen to the radio, cassettes, or CDs. The exception is when the decibel level is so high that your concentration is impaired (or you don't hear that ambulance).

Exercising with a Walkman isn't terrible, but it's not the greatest. At my health club recently, I was bemused to see a lady who was not only on the stair-climber with a Walkman, but she then opened a book and started to read. I almost asked if she wanted to chew some gum, to see whether she could do four things at once.

The physical exercises in which you engage are ideally their own reward. Still, I know many people who use workout exercise tapes, or get on a stationary bike while watching a movie or basketball on television. It seems to work well for them, so there's probably no real harm.

Other activities where it's okay to double up include the following: walking and talking with a friend, taking notes as you listen to a lecture, and talking to your lover while you're having sex (depending on your partner, this can enhance the experience).

The Least You Need to Know

➤ The more often you can get into the habit of doing one thing at a time, the better you'll do, and the more time will slow down for you.

➤ The most accomplished people in history acted with urgency, but they were not in a hurry—they didn't walk faster, talk faster, or try to speed up other bodily functions.

➤ If you've been multitasking for a long time, going cold turkey and handling one thing at a time may cause anxiety. This is natural; you'll have to ease into it.

➤ Among the many exercises you may try, get into the habit of doing one thing at a time. Promise yourself you'll go for 10 minutes on a task the first day, 15 the second, and so forth.

➤ Most of the areas where it's okay to double up on activities are outside the workplace.

➤ You don't need to be entertained as much as you think.

Chapter 16

The Urge to Merge and Purge

In This Chapter

➤ Looking for ways to streamline your life

➤ Examining high-priority areas of your life, one at a time

➤ How to pare down a little each day

➤ How to uncomplicate your systems

Now you're making hay. So far in Part 3, you've learned how to make big decisions in record time (Chapter 14) and the magic of doing one thing at a time (Chapter 15). Now you're ready to learn about merging and purging—clearing out what you don't need so you can have more of a "life" each day.

Merging and purging files (and other things you're hanging on to) is more than good housekeeping; it's an emerging discipline among winners in society today. It's essential because even with all the new high-tech tools, paper will continue to mushroom for the foreseeable future. When I speak to groups I tell them that once you let go of all that stuff you're holding on to, you will experience the same reward as a good garage cleaning or unblocking that backed-up plumbing. You're free!

Merge and Purge or Be Doomed

Consider all you encounter in the course of a day, week, month, and year—faxes, memos, reports, newspapers, newsletters, bulletins, magazines, bills, calendars, promotional items, and that's just the beginning. How would your life be if you merged and purged these items on a regular basis as they came into your life? Well, for one thing, you'd have far more time. Why? Because accumulations by their nature rob you of your time. First you receive them, then put them somewhere, look at them, move them, attempt to arrange them, file some items, discard others, try in vain to find the items you need, and then put up your hands and say, "I can't win."

You know you're hanging on to too much stuff and it's slowing you down. When are the best times to merge and purge what you've retained? Try these on for size:

➤ Anytime you approach a birthday is a good time, particularly a zero-year birthday. If you're about to hit 40, this is one of the great times in life to get rid of the stuff you no longer need. Age 30, age 50, and age 60 will work as well.

➤ New Year's is a good time, especially if it's the change of a decade—a zero year such as the year 2000.

➤ Merge and purge right after you've filed your taxes. If you procrastinate (and a lot of people do when it comes to taxes), not to worry. After you've finished filing there are all kinds of benefits. For one, you can get rid of most receipts and documents from the tax year three years prior to the one you completed. The law says you have to hang on to the forms filed, but not the nitty-gritty details. (If you've been audited, or you anticipate problems with the IRS, that's a different story.)

➤ Spring cleaning has traditionally been a time for clearing out the old and making room for the new. The arrival of fall works as well, toward the end of the summer around Labor Day.

➤ Merge and purge when you move. There's no sense in paying the movers to haul stuff to your new location that you're never going to use anyway.

➤ When you change jobs or careers, you'll have to clean out your old desk at work. That's usually a given.

➤ Passing one of life's milestones—the birth of a child, the death of a parent, graduation, retirement, getting a major raise, and anything on that order—can often serve as a reminder to reexamine what you're retaining. Rearrange it to accommodate the new you.

➤ Any time the spirit moves you is a good time to merge and purge.

➤ As you finish reading *this particular paragraph*, I give you permission to put down the book and actually go ahead and merge and purge some area of your life. Make it an easy win, something you can tackle and master in 10 to 15 minutes.

Examine the Compartments of Your Life

When you don't feel in control of your time, everything in your life may seem as if it's running together into one big blur. Thus the easiest way to approach merging and purging is to examine the most important compartments of your life, one at a time.

Examine your desk and what needs to be there, then your entire office, then where you live, your car, and other important areas of your life. Here are some suggestions:

➤ Do you have a file folder, a notebook or a magazine box holder where you keep all travel-related materials? This might include booklets on hotel and air fares, frequent-flyer numbers, passports, numbers for taxis, and other transportation, and vacation club folders. I keep such phone and membership numbers in one long file on my hard disk; a printout in a small point size tucks into my portable appointment calendar. Wherever I am, day or night, I have the information I need.

I've maintained such a list for more than 12 years now and no one has ever gotten hold of it. The power and efficiency it gives me is awesome. Whether I'm at an airport, in a taxi, at a hotel or phone booth, I have all the phone numbers, membership numbers, card numbers, codes—everything I need to stay efficiently in motion. Is this a fabulous time-saver? Major, major hint: The answer begins with "Y."

➤ You can undertake the same type of exercise in merging and purging items at your desk when it comes to key service providers, records related to your automobile, insurance forms and policies, banking information, and other areas where efficiency matters. In all cases it takes a little time to merge and purge what you've retained and get it into a streamlined, highly useable form. Once you do, watch out—your efficiency level is going to soar.

Warning
If you're worried that someone might come upon your list of membership numbers and the like, you can always code it so that the first one or two digits are bogus (or disguise it as a phone number for a club name you've made up).

➤ The same maneuvers can be undertaken around your office. What can be consolidated, reduced, eliminated, relocated, or donated? Is your office configuration serving you best? Do you need to move things (knowing what you now know) to improve your daily efficiency? Can hardcopy items be scanned to see if they're now on disk and you no longer need the hard copy? If you have four stacking trays, can you reduce the number to three? Do you even need an in-basket anymore?

➤ At home, if you maintain a desk or any type of home office, reapply all these methods and go a step further. For example, could you use a 31-day tickler file in your *home* desk as well as the one you use in your office? If you use scheduling software at work, do you need to update your system at home?

Can you consolidate family-related records so that you're in greater control? For example, all of Johnny's documents related to grade-school enrollment, immunization, early-school-dismissal policy, and summer camp could be put in the same three-ring binder. All records related to your car (purchase documents, registration, tax information, inspections passed, repair records, special installations such as a CD player, and so on) could fit into one file.

What a Concept!

It's better to keep your car records in your home office if that's where you make phone calls and payments concerning your car. You can always keep a backup of much of the documentation discussed here, buried someplace deep in your car's trunk.

➤ Your car is also an important area of your life and, based on what may have accumulated, requires merging and purging as well. Can you get all of your credit cards, library cards, and the like into a secondary wallet to be hidden someplace in the car? I do this, rather than carrying a wallet with 25 different cards in it. Why? Because at any given moment, the only cards I actually need are my driver's license, one ATM card, and one credit card.

Any time I might use one of the other cards, I'm usually with my car. By safely stashing the cards I would only use with my car someplace within the car, I free myself from carrying all of them. This has several time-saving advantages. One, you're less likely to lose a majority of your cards if you lose your wallet. Two, it's far easier to find your license, major credit card, and ATM card, if they are the only ones you carry in your wallet.

As a safeguard you might want to copy all your credit cards and library cards on a copier, and keep a backup sheet at home and hidden in your car. *(If cars disappear frequently in your neighborhood, skip this one!)*

I also find it a great time-saver to have all my maps in one place, within reach, while driving. I use side pockets built into the driver's-side and passenger's-side front doors. You may use your glove compartment, a compartment between your two front seats, the trunk, or whatever space you have. Essentials such as car registration and proof of ownership stay snug at the bottom of my glove compartment.

What a Concept!

An easy way to organize lots of little items is to use individual envelopes, small, clear, plastic sandwich bags, or zip-lock baggies. This enables you to see what's inside, and keeps the items dry and together.

Half the trouble of staying in control of your time is staying in control of your possessions. I mean, let's face it—there's so much you have to keep tabs on, it could almost be a full-time job in itself. If you're willing to occasionally kill one Saturday morning getting these systems into place, you'll find that the payoffs come back to you over and over again.

Paring Down a Little at a Time

Don't attempt to tackle all arenas of your life on the *same* Saturday morning. Not only will you not finish, but the process itself may scare you away for a year or more.

Try these ways to pare down a little at a time without breaking your stride:

➤ Any time you're waiting for someone at work, at home, or in your car, use the extra few minutes to pare down something where you are. If you have to drive your children around town a lot, after a few days you ought to have your car whipped into shape.

➤ When you've finished a big project at work and you're not ready to tackle some other major, intellectual pursuit at the moment, pare down your holdings as a form of transition. For example, if you recently finished a big report, can you now delete previous versions on your hard disk? Can you get rid of rough drafts and notes that are no longer applicable (notes you'll never use again)?

Warning
If you're high on the prospect of streamlining your life, then you've got to think about paring down a little at a time; there is no other way. You already *have* a full-time job and a raft of responsibilities.

CAUTION

➤ If your plans go awry because it's raining, the bridge is out, or the plane has been delayed for an hour, pare down. Despite the availability of all manner of electronic gadgetry at your seat on the plane, I know high-powered executives who will have none of it. Their seats in airplanes, they tell me, are *among the few sanctuaries they have*. It's where they get to open their briefcases and impose some order, merging and purging, updating lists, chucking what's no longer necessary, and getting that little office-in-the-air back in shape.

➤ The same holds true if you commute by rail or bus. Use the little moments of the day to pare down. Instead of lugging around whole issues of *Forbes*, *Business Week*, or *Working Woman*, fly through them like wildfire and extract only the articles that look relevant. Leave the rest for the next passenger or drop it at the next recycling bin. Stay light.

One Less Form to Answer

A stifling array of government laws and regulations hamper business, allowing the U.S. to support 70% of the world's lawyers, says Barry Howard Minkin in *EconoQuake*. Thus, it becomes vitally important for you, a mere pawn in the game of laws and regulations, to keep your own systems as uncomplicated as possible. It won't be easy—there is a pervasive tendency among organizations and individuals to overcomplicate their lives. You can see its effects every time you fill out your tax forms.

Are the forms getting any easier to fill out each year despite the IRS's long-term commitment to simplifying them, or are they getting more difficult? Have you bought any property recently? Are there more forms, or fewer? Without question, there are more. Some states have double the number they had ten years ago.

> **Warning**
> All too often in the business world, if you *can* create a new reporting form, you do. Thereafter it becomes difficult to eliminate. If anything, such forms get longer, more complicated, and more time-intensive.

If you're an entrepreneur, or if you supervise others, think about the last time you tried to fire someone. Is it getting harder or easier from the standpoint of completing paperwork?

Your mission, if you decide to accept it, is to look at the forms you've created in your organization, department, or venture, and re-examine them—what can be eliminated? Here are some advantages you might experience from eliminating a single form:

Immediate benefits:

➤ Paper: Less ordering, fewer costs, less receiving, less handling, and less storing.

➤ Printing: Less retrieving, less printer use, less electricity, lower cartridge and toner costs, or lower outside costs if purchased by a printer or forms vender.

➤ Storing: Less collecting, less transporting, less storage space used, less employee time used up.

➤ Distributing: Less retrieving, less disseminating.

Benefits for those who must complete the form:

➤ Completing: Less writing, less handling, less ink.

➤ Submitting: Less walking, less faxing, less mailing or e-mailing.

Benefits for those who must deal with the completed form:

➤ Collecting: Less walking, less opening mail, less handling faxes.

➤ Compiling: Less sorting, less calculating, less totaling.

➤ Reporting: Less writing, less presenting, less mental energy expended.

Uncomplicating Your Own Systems

Months ago I was called by a marketing representative from a well-established investment company. Usually I listen to them for a minute and then find a polite way to end the conversation. This particular caller seemed to know his subject well, so I listened and even responded. He talked about his company's various investment options and told me that he could send a brochure listing the 35 different investment vehicles that they had available, plus his company's annual report and prospectus.

"Wait a second," I told him, "I have no interest in reading about 35 different investment options. Please, do me and yourself a favor by boiling down your information to a single page. Then send a paragraph on the three options that you think would be best for me." I also told him I was not going to read his company's annual report, so there was no reason to send it.

If I liked what he sent me on the single page, I could always get the annual report at another time. I told him that while I'm an MBA, am certified as a management

consultant, and have worked with hundreds of companies, "I'm not fond of reading prospectuses, so please don't send that either."

At the end of our conversation, I repeated to him that I only needed to see a single page with the three investments he thought were best for me—and perhaps one slim brochure on his company.

Several days passed, and I forgot about the call. When Monday's mail came I noticed a thick package from his investment house. I cringed. I opened it, and voilà— a brochure on the 35 investment vehicles, an annual and a quarterly report, the company's thick prospectus, and other useless brochures and fliers. I grabbed the pile and tried to rip the whole thing with one flick of my wrists, but it was too thick. I tossed it and (rest assured) did not become a client.

If that broker had sent me what I asked for, who knows, I might have made his day.

The Replacement Principle

When you boil it down, uncomplicating your own systems is synonymous with getting into a replacement mode. When you take in something new, something else has to go. Table 16.1 offers some everyday examples of non-replacement policies (left column) contrasted with replacement policies (right column).

Table 16.1 The Replacement Principle

Non-Replacement Policies	Replacement Policy
Your child's collection of videos grows to beyond 50 as you buy or copy the classic and latest hits.	You decide with your child in advance on a total number of videos (s)he can have. Each new one means replacing an old one.
Your file cabinet keeps growing until you need to buy another.	Your files stay the same size; for each item you add, you discard one.

Non-Replacement Policies	Replacement Policy
You keep old equipment in closets and storage bins, thinking it'll come in handy.	As soon as you buy new equipment, you donate the old equipment to a charity and get a tax deduction.
You've collected books for years and now have no hope of reading what's on the overflowing shelves.	You retain only books of continuing or sentimental value, scanning most for important info and giving them away.
You have a 560-megabyte hard disk, and are considering getting more disk space.	You don't need more disk space because you prune your disk of outdated files at least once a month.
You have an unread collection of annual reports, and other items from investment houses.	An investment firm sends you an annual report; right away you replace last year's.
Your clothes drawers and closets are overfilled with items you haven't worn in years.	There's plenty of space in the house for clothes you actually use; you give the rest to charities.

If you're not constantly reducing what you hold on to, you're at the dubious mercy of an era that keeps throwing more at you than you can respond to. Seize control of your time—merge and purge and then go splurge!

The Least You Need to Know

➤ Merging and purging what you're retaining is an emerging discipline among winners in society today.

➤ The best reminders to pare down are a birthday, a change of year or season, one of life's milestones, or anytime you have the spirit to do so.

➤ Pare down a little at a time; biting off too much may tempt you to think it's hopeless, when it's not.

➤ Examine your work environment to determine what forms can be eliminated. It all counts.

➤ Uncomplicate your own systems by *not* volunteering to be inundated by junk mail and irrelevant stuff; rely on the replacement principle.

Part 4
Peace-of-Mind Goals

You're making great progress! You're all the way up to Part 4. When you first bought this book, you worried that you might not make it this far, didn't you?

You've been following a progression. In Part 1, you learned specific techniques for making the most of your day. In Part 2, you learned about the importance of controlling your environment, getting enough sleep, whipping your office into shape, filing, and using the tools of technology. In Part 3, you refined your capabilities further by learning to make decisions quickly, practicing the art of doing one thing at a time, and lightening the load by merging and purging.

Now it's time to move into that wondrous and potentially serene arena—your head—to discuss goals for peace of mind. This is where you learn to become a master of winning back your time through deciding to live in real time, catching up with today, dropping back and punting, and realizing that the best is yet to come.

Get ready for the stratosphere. Fear not—you are ready. First up, is deciding to live in real time (as opposed to what you've been living in—preoccupied time).

Chapter 17

Deciding to Live in Real Time

> **In This Chapter**
>
> ➤ Locked up in preoccupied time? Here's a key...
>
> ➤ What *real* time is, and what it's like being there
>
> ➤ Twelve measures to help you live in *real* time

In your quest to keep pace with all that's thrown at you, it's a good bet you're frequently preoccupied. You don't enjoy lunch because you're worried about what needs to be done in the afternoon. You don't enjoy the afternoon because you're thinking about how you have to pick up your child, get across town to attend a meeting, and then get back. You don't enjoy the evening because it goes by too fast. You don't enjoy the morning because you're always in a rush, concerned about getting to work on time. Perhaps that's the *old* you because the first sixteen chapters have actually sunk in. I hope so.

What Is Real Time?

How would your life be if you could tackle problems and challenges as they arise? What would it feel like to engage in conceptual thinking whenever you wanted or needed to? If you had a sense of control and ease about each day? The short answer: You would be living in *real time*.

Being There: Go for Completion

Steve Sugar, formerly a program planner at the National Institute of Health in Bethesda, Maryland, carries a task to completion instead of leaving it for later (when it might be one of a growing pile of tasks, requiring additional effort). Sugar finds that even if it doesn't "feel good," sticking with the task at hand is one of the most effective ways of staying in real time and getting things off your desk, be it fielding a phone call, returning correspondence, or working on a budget.

Diane Weems, an executive with the North Carolina Travel Association, finds that one of her core strategies for effectiveness is to take phone calls *when they come in* (as often as possible), rather than let them pile up. In essence, she uses the technique of *completion* to focus on the task at hand, pause, answer the phone, handle the call, and resume work. She's honed the ability to switch quickly from one task to another—and each is the *one* task she's engaged in at the time.

By taking phone calls as they come in, she can interact with the caller to resolve the issue, often within the duration of the call. "When you let the number of return calls you have to make build up beyond a certain level," Weems says, "you ensure that you won't get back to all the callers, and you're going to procrastinate when it comes to calling many of them."

Weems also finds it useful to deal with mail and papers that come across her desk as they arrive, but concedes that this isn't always possible.

You may know people who live in real time or at least live out significant chunks of their lives in real time. Who are these people? If you know someone who stays in shape, has the time to take a phone call, and actually knows each of his or her children's friends *by name*, you've got a clue. The person who volunteers for—and takes an active role in—community organizations is probably living in real time.

Twelve Components of Living in Real Time

Going for completion, handling phone calls as they come in, and finishing the task at hand are worthwhile achievements—and these elements of life are within your potential. Take a look at the following twelve components of living in real time, with the realization that each of these are within your grasp.

1. **Leave home in the morning with grace and ease.** As you know from Chapter 11, you can manage the beforehand. Take care of as many things as possible the night before, so that in the morning you have only to get bodies out the door. No need for a mad rush; you've got everything ready to go.

2. **Focus on the important issues facing your organization, your department or division, your job or career.** As you learned in Chapter 6's discussion about priorities, you have to pay homage to the issues that you identify as important in your life, and have the strength to ignore the also-rans. Magically, when you take care of the important things, the others fall into place.

3. **Handle and deal with the day's mail upon arrival, keep piles from forming on your desk, and handle phone calls within 24 hours.** If you practice the techniques discussed in Chapters 12 and 13, your skills will be enhanced in all these areas. No need to be inundated by the mail; no piles that accumulate on your desk; no snarl of phone calls to get back to.

4. **Enjoy a leisurely lunch.** From Chapter 15, you know the importance of completing tasks so that when you go to lunch, you're *at lunch*. You get to chew slowly and carefully. You give up reading the newspaper, and focus on the food in your mouth. Old sensations may return. You actually enjoy your lunch, digest your food better, do better back on the job, and have a vastly improved gastrointestinal outlook. Can you beat it?

   Van VanDyck, Education Manager with American Express in Phoenix, insists on having lunch *away from his desk*. By getting away from the office, VanDyck is able to recharge his batteries. He feels that when you stay at your desk too long, every task competing for your attention, big and small, seems too urgent. By getting away at lunchtime, VanDyck is able to stay focused on the big picture. He can return to the office with newfound energy.

5. **Depart from the workplace at normal closing hours and feel good about what you accomplish each day.** This is straight from Chapter Numero Uno; leaving the workday on time and complete is the single most important step you can take toward permanently winning back your time. Ask yourself, "What do I need to accomplish by the end of the day to feel good about leaving on time?" You'll hardly ever leave defeated or in a bad mood.

6. **Have sufficient and up-to-date health, life, disability, and automobile insurance coverage.** If you want to live in real time, this is part of the overall picture. Following the discussion of priorities in Chapter 6, getting adequate insurance to protect you and your loved ones is bound to support your overall priorities.

7. **File your annual (and any quarterly) income taxes on time.** For tax year 1994, IRS records indicate that more than 40% of taxpayers filed for extensions; they did not need to send in their completed tax returns until August 15, or in some cases October 15. You, on the other hand (once you've decided to live in real time), recognize that taxes are a necessary evil and will always be levied. You set up a tax log at the start of each year with room for each legitimate deduction, where you can file receipts and documentation. Perhaps you buy software such as Turbo Tax or Quicken that helps you to complete your tax returns on a timely basis.

8. **Take time to be with friends and relatives.** People, not things, count most in this life. Remembering your priorities and supporting goals, becoming adept at making decisions, you gain the power to carve out time in your schedule to ensure that you don't short-change the people who are central in your life.

9. **Stay in shape and at your desired weight.** When you observe the bodies of most individuals, you can see the results of a losing tug-of-war with gravity. Body parts seem to be down from prior years, but gravity need not win this round. Health and fitness experts say that working out for as little as 30 minutes a day, four times a week, can keep you comfortably fit. As I observed in my book *Breathing Space: Living and Working at a Comfortable Pace in a Sped-Up Society*, if you're too busy to stay in shape, you're too busy!

10. **Make time for hobbies.** On the way to *losing* your time, did you abandon enjoyable activities that were a part of what made you who you are? I thought so. Revisit that stamp collection, garden, hiking club, or whatever you let slide. Living in real time means enjoying your most rewarding hobbies and pastimes *regularly*.

11. **Participate monthly in a worthy cause.** As you learned in Chapter 9, it's not possible to give your time and attention to all worthy causes, or even many. Your life is finite, regardless of how long you live. When you pick the one or two that matter most to you and take action, you feel good about yourself and about how you're spending your time.

    Some factors that increase the probability of your paying homage to these causes include: not having to travel too far to participate, enjoying your co-participants, getting a psychological boost (an internal reward) and recognition for your efforts (external rewards) when you participate.

12. **Drop back at any time, take a long deep breath, collect your thoughts, and renew your spirit—the focus of the remaining chapters.**

How Many Can You Actualize?

It's great to have lists of all the things you're going to do, but lists alone are useless unless you take *action*.

Several of the ways to live in real time discussed in the preceding section may appeal to you. Suppose you wanted to actualize #9, staying in shape and at your desired weight. How would you *actually* succeed?

From Chapter 5 and Chapter 6, you learned that any goal you set needs to be specific and time-related. One of the first things you might do is commit to working out regularly, and determine what you'll weigh by a certain date. From Chapter 14, you learned that you don't need to surround yourself with reams of data and analysis before taking action—although some information may be worthwhile—your intuition is up and running. Use it too.

Plan your changes gradually. In the first week you could decide that you'll no longer eat in your car. In the next few weeks you'll stop eating when watching television. Thereafter, you might substitute skim milk for whole milk, stop putting butter on your potatoes, and so forth.

The point is, after you pick one of the twelve measures of living in real time (or some other measure that's important to you), create a six-, eight-, or ten-step action plan. Based on the measure you choose and the particular circumstances of your life, your plan will be different from someone else's. The keys to making your plan work are to follow the goal reinforcement techniques discussed in Chapter 6, some of which are briefly summarized here:

> **Warning**
> How many times have you encountered people around New Year's who have made all kinds of resolutions, but who can't remember any of them by January 8? Why do they bother?!

➤ Seek others with goals similar to yours.

➤ Post reinforcing statements and reminders in view.

➤ Record affirming statements on cassette.

➤ Determine any cash outlays in advance.

➤ Take bite-size action steps.

➤ Have someone waiting to hear of your progress.

➤ Envision yourself succeeding.

➤ Plot your plan on the calendar starting from the end date.

➤ Build in some flexibility.

What a Concept!

The plan will work best if you can initiate a part of it every day.

The Least You Need to Know

➤ Start leaving your home each morning with relative grace and ease because of steps you took the night before to ensure it.

➤ Take time to be with and enjoy friends and relatives, and to re-engage in your hobbies. These are strong self-indications that you're in control of your time.

➤ Devise a realistic action plan that ensures you will master *one* of the important measures of living in real time. Thereafter, tackle another, and then another.

186

Chapter 18

Catching Up with Today (or at Least with This Week?)

In This Chapter

➤ No one is holding a whip behind you

➤ When you're in motion, it's easy to *feel* productive, but true productivity is measured by results

➤ By *lingering* at crucial moments throughout the day, you can reclaim control of your day

➤ Find out why overly hard-driving types are rarely as productive in the long run as those who pace themselves

Once you realize what it means to live in real time—and how far you've strayed from the mark—there are several things you can do to begin to catch up with today (or at least this week). Many of them are deceptively simple, but don't let that obscure the powerful results they offer.

No One Is Holding a Whip Behind You

As I travel around the country speaking to organizations, I am struck by the number of people in my audiences who seem perpetually overwhelmed. The irony is that though these people *could* take breaks throughout their days and weeks, they don't. The biggest obstacle to winning back your time is the *unwillingness to allow yourself a break*.

I spoke to one group of executives and their spouses, and learned from many spouses that their executive husbands or wives simply do not allow themselves to take a break. Paradoxically, increasing evidence indicates that executives will be more effective if they pause for an extra minute a couple of times each day. This can be done every morning and afternoon—when returning from the water cooler or restroom, before leaving for lunch, when returning from lunch, and that's just the short list.

> ### What a Concept!
>
> Seven hours and fifty minutes of work *plus ten one-minute intervals of rest or reflection* in a workday, will make you more productive than eight solid hours of work.

To insist on proceeding full-speed through the day, without allowing yourself ten minutes to clear your mind, all but guarantees you'll be less effective than those who do. Even the people who already perceive this need do not let themselves meet it.

To Stay Competitive

The Motorola Corporation discovered the hard way that a little instruction here and there didn't educate their employees the way they had hoped, and certainly didn't stick with their employees. Motorola now has its own university with its own staff of 300 instructors and a $60,000,000 annual budget. They have also developed in-house programs and long-term alliances with local colleges.

Go!
Have you taken the time to map your own times of maximum and minimum alertness during your typical workday? The information is vital.

Why such elaborate procedures? To help the organization stay competitive. Similarly, for *you* to stay competitive, you need to pause periodically throughout the day—every day.

Some of the most productive and energetic people in history learned how to pace themselves effectively by taking a few "time outs" each day. Thomas Edison would rest for a few minutes each day when he felt his energy level dropping. Buckminster Fuller often worked in cycles of three or four hours, slept for 30 minutes, and then repeated the process. He found that in the course of a twenty-four hour period, he would get far more done than in the traditional waking and sleeping pattern. By giving himself rest at shorter intervals, Fuller was able to extend his productive hours.

Remember, the time for *most* people when they are least alert is between 2:00 a.m. and 5:00 a.m. Highest alertness is between 9:00 a.m. and noon, and 4:00 p.m. to 8:00 p.m. Your alertness will vary depending on your own physiology and inclinations, as well as on the hours of consecutive duty, hours of duty in the preceding week, irregular hours, monotony on the job, timing and duration of naps, environmental lighting, sound, aroma, temperature, cumulative sleep deprivation over the past week, and much more.

> **Warning**
> Applying the measures discussed here in a hit-or-miss, now-and-then way *won't* give you a sense of control over your day, afford you greater peace of mind, or enable you to win back your time. Give the quest your commitment.

Strategic Pauses Every Day

You'd think that entrepreneurs, running their own businesses and managing themselves, would be more inclined to take strategic pauses throughout the day—after all, they're in charge of their own schedule. Too often, it isn't necessarily so; the temptation to overwork can be ferocious. Conversely, if you work for others, perhaps a large organization, you may erroneously believe that if you pause for the total of ten strategic minutes throughout a workday it would somehow jeopardize your standing. This misconception is unfounded.

> **What a Concept!**
> The CEOs in many top organizations routinely take naps at mid-day to recharge their batteries. They have executive assistants who shield them from the outside world, take their calls, and arrange their schedules.

If you are *not* the CEO of a large organization, the thought of being able to take a nap in the middle of the workday may seem like Nirvana to you. Yet the ten strategic minutes I have recommended provide a similar benefit. If you can't take a flat-out nap, ten strategic minutes may be your best alternative.

Vanishing Laughter

How many times do you actually let out a good laugh during the day, especially the work day? Five-year-olds reportedly laugh 113 times a day on average. 44-year-olds laugh only 11 times per day. Something happens between the ages of five and forty-four that reduces the chuckle factor.

Go!
Step back and see the humor in your life; laughter gives you a break in the action, makes things less tense, and puts you back in control.

Once you reach retirement, fortunately, you tend to laugh again. The trick is to live and work at a comfortable pace and have a lot of laughs along the way—at every age. When you proceed through the workday without humor, the days tend to be long and difficult. Part of taking control of your life is being able to step back and look at the big picture—being able to see the humorous, lighter side of things. Some of your worst gaffes eventually evolve into the things you pleasantly recall—or your best ideas! Pros who survive, laugh.

When Your Mind Hurts

I told my little girl, Valerie, that my sister is a doctor—but not a doctor of the body, a doctor of the mind. Valerie promptly asked, "Does she check your mind by opening your head?" I told her no. Valerie then asked, "Do you make an appointment to see her when your mind hurts?" Out of the mouths of babes! I said yes. Valerie finally said, "Sometimes my mind hurts when I cry too much." And so it is with grown-ups whose minds hurt when they try to *take in* too much, *work* too much, and *be* too much.

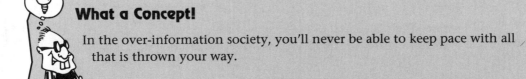

What a Concept!
In the over-information society, you'll never be able to keep pace with all that is thrown your way.

You have to let the anxiety pass that comes from walking past the rack with hundreds of issues of magazines. You need to let the stress subside when you walk into a bookstore to pick out *one* book on your topic from the 80 available, or when you receive so many sales promotions, discounts, and bonus offers in the mail that you can't read all of them, let alone absorb or take advantage of them. Let them pass.

Winning Back Your Time: Today and Tomorrow

The Winning Back Your Time Worksheet in this chapter includes ten activities: five at work, three after work, and two during vacation time. Each of these activities has a "Lately," "Short-Term Goal," and "Long-Term Goal" category. In the Lately column, enter how many times in the past month you have actually done each activity. In each Goal column, enter how many times you would like to, say, take a slow and leisurely lunch. In the short-term goal category, for example, you could indicate two times per week.

Be realistic when recording what you have been doing. Be reflective in the short-term goal column, marking down what you can realistically achieve. Be visionary in the long-term goal column, marking down what you would ideally like to achieve.

Worksheet for Winning Back Your Time At Work: Today and Tomorrow

Time:	Lately	Short-Term Goal	Long-Term Goal
Extra minute taken daily			
Leisurely lunches per week			
Hours per week in non-rush mode			
Full weekends you take off per month			

Worksheet for Winning Back Your Time After Work: Today and Tomorrow

Time:	Lately	Short-Term Goal	Long-Term Goal
Days per month using alternate way home			
Days per month you have fun on the way home			
Days per month telecommuting from home			

Worksheet for Winning Back Your Vacation Time: Today and Tomorrow

Time:	Last 12 Months	Next 12 Months	Three Years from Now
3- to 4-day vacations you take annually			
Week-long vacations you take annually			

In the weeks and months ahead, review your chart weekly for reinforcement. You need to be taking breaks like these throughout the day, week, and year. I don't know who else is going to tell you this, and I don't know how you're going to make yourself do it unless you systematize the procedure.

The advice to take periodic breaks seems so simple, yet you may find it difficult to put into practice. It reminds me of lyrics from that song by The Who, "I'm Free":

"If I told you what it takes to reach the highest high,
You'd laugh and say that nothing's that simple.
But you've been told many times before,
Messiahs pointed to the door
And no one had the guts to leave the temple."

Shaking Up Your Routine

Sometimes, in the quest to catch up with today, shaking up some of your time-honored routines can help. For example:

➤ **Get up one hour earlier.** Thirty-five years ago, the concept of "late night" (11:00 p.m.) news was unknown. People went to bed at 9:30 or 10:00. Once people began staying up for the late news, the networks began running late-night talk shows. As a result, the entire population is staying up later than the previous generation.

➤ **Work on the porch of your house instead of in the office.** As you've learned throughout the book, when you change your venue and the scenery, you open up new vistas. Alternatively, work under a tree or at a pool during nice weather. Being near nature opens up a way of viewing things that you cannot get in the office. When working in a natural, tranquil setting, you'll gain peace of mind in your otherwise-hectic work routine. When you do this for some of your tasks (especially tasks that require conceptualization or creative thinking), you'll be more productive than ever before.

As the author of 20 books, I find that I proofread much better on the porch or in a swing than when I'm at my desk. Begin to identify the places in your life that are welcome retreats to go and work—a library, even sitting in your car in a shopping-center parking lot. When you change where you're working, you can benefit immensely and immediately.

➤ **Drop the unproductive 80 percent of your activities.** The Pareto Principle (the "80/20" rule) states that 80 percent of your activities contribute to only 20 percent of your results.

Go!
As recommended in Chapter 6, why not go to bed earlier and wake up an hour earlier? In that extra hour, you can watch the sun rise, meditate, do some exercises, or go to work before traffic gets bad. The activities you undertake in that early hour can affect your perspective on the whole day. To get a fresh perspective, shake up your routine and get up earlier!

The remaining 20 percent of your activities contribute to the other 80 percent of your results. Take a hardware store for example: about 20 percent of its stock accounts for 80 percent of the revenues; the remaining 80 percent of the stock accounts for only 20 percent of the revenues.

The key to successful retailing is identifying the 20 percent producing the bulk of the revenues. A smart store manager knows to place that 20 percent where it's most accessible, and put the rest where it won't get in the way. As you learned in Chapter 6, you need to identify which activities in your work (and personal life) support you and bring you the best results. Have the strength to abandon activities that don't benefit you—get rid of that unproductive 80 percent.

➤ **Ask for input.** Have you ever gone to lunch with a colleague and begun discussing ways to approach your work more effectively? After a few minutes you're both deep into the conversation, coming up with all sorts of great ideas. However, when the waiter comes to take your order or bring your check, what happens? The conversation dies down.

When you both go back to work, those ideas are often forgotten or put on a back burner. If you consciously schedule a meeting for the sole purpose of letting the creative sparks fly, you'll grab control of your time and have some of the most productive sessions you've ever had.

I meet with a mentor once a month in his dining room. At a cleared table, we sit across from each other with tape recorders, discussing problems and issues that face us and ways we can overcome them. Each of us keeps a copy of the tape, takes it home, and makes notes on it. We *capture* those ideas instead of letting them die.

> ## What a Concept!
>
> When you come in contact with other people, you're exposed to *whole new worlds*—their worlds. When you interact with another person, you get the benefit of her information, in addition to your own.

Look for other ways to shake up your routine for the insights and breakthroughs that may result—every day and every moment holds great potential.

"Slowing Down" Time

You may be thinking, "Yeah, if each minute holds so much potential, how come they still race by so fast?" The way you experience time passing each day is based on your perception. You can slow down time if you choose. How? Whenever you feel you're racing the clock or trying to tackle too much at once, try this exercise:

> Close your eyes for a minute and imagine a pleasant scene. It could be in nature or with a loved one. It could be something from childhood. Let the emotions of that place and time predominate. Get into it! Give yourself more than a New York minute for the visualization to take hold. Then open your eyes and return to what you're doing. What you're working on is not quite so bad; the pace you were working at is not quite so feverish.

One effective method for catching up with today is periodically deleting three items from your "to-do list" *without doing them at all*. Before you shriek, consider that much of what makes your list is arbitrary. If you can eliminate three, in most cases it will have no impact on your career or life, except for freeing up a little time for yourself in the present. Nice gift.

Reflect

Think about flying on an airplane. You have a window seat, and it's a clear day. As you gaze down to the ground below, what do you see? Life passing by. Cars the size of ants. Miniature baseball diamonds. Rivers the size of streams.

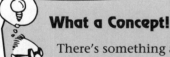

What a Concept!

There's something about being at great heights that enables you to reflect on your life.

The same phenomenon can take place at the top of a mountain, or a skyscraper. As often as possible, when things seems to be racing by too fast, get to higher ground for a clear perspective. If you're among the lucky, perhaps you regularly allocate time for reflection or meditation. If you don't, no matter—there are other ways to slow it all down. After the workday, really *listen* to relaxing music with headphones on and with your eyes closed. A half hour of your favorite music with no disturbances (and your eyes closed) can seem almost endless. When you re-emerge, the rest of the day takes on a different (ahem) tenor.

Rely on the Animal Kingdom

If you have a dog or cat and do not consider it a drain on your time, here's a little something about Rover or Mittens that you may not have known. In recent years, as reported by *U.S. News & World Report*, scientists have found proof for what was only suspected: that contact with animals has specific and measurable effects on both your body and mind. The mere presence of animals can increase a sick person's chances of survival, and has been shown to lower heart rate, calm disturbed children, and induce incommunicative people to initiate conversation!

What a Concept!

The exact mechanisms that animals exert to affect your health and well-being are still largely mysterious. Scientists suspect that animal companionship is beneficial because, *unlike human interaction* (!), it is uncomplicated.

Animals are nonjudgmental, accepting, and attentive; they don't talk back, criticize, or give orders. Animals have a unique capacity to draw people out.

Even if you only have goldfish, sometimes simply staring at them in their silent world can help slow your pace. Some folks find watching fish restful.

The Least You Need to Know

➤ Allow yourself to take breaks so you can relieve unnecessary pressures and catch up with today.

➤ Pause for ten separate minutes each day. The happiest and most productive people give themselves the extra minute here and there throughout the day.

➤ Whenever you choose, take a deep breath, get balanced, clear your head, glide back in your chair, or look out the window.

➤ Up your laugh quotient: Look for the humor in situations.

➤ Sometimes, in the quest to catch up with today, shaking up some of your time-honored routines can help.

Chapter 19

Drop Back and Punt—Periodically Abandoning the Rat Race

In This Chapter

➤ Why it's getting harder (*and more crucial*) to take a break from your normal work routine

➤ You have the ability to retrain and recharge yourself!

➤ How to get new references in your life

➤ How to take a personal sabbatical

Can you withdraw from the maddening crowd? I'm talking about going whole weekends without doing anything, taking *true* vacations, and spending evenings sitting on the porch, as the late John Lennon said, "watching the wheels go round and round." These are not lost arts. Nevertheless, if you've spent too many anxiety-ridden days in a row—say, ten years' worth—or maintained some monomaniacal quest to fill up every minute with meaningful or worthwhile activities, your task is cut out for you. This chapter can help.

Why It's Getting Harder to Take a Break

The great paradox of being an ambitious professional functioning in an over-information society, is that you tend to keep doing what you're doing. If you're working too long, trying to keep pace, and taking in more and more information, the impetus is for you to keep doing that; even when it isn't satisfying or healthy.

Anyone can fall into this trap—it's human nature. As your responsibilities mount at work, you may actually find yourself dreading the notion of taking a vacation because of all the work that would pile up when you're away. (Sound too familiar? Thought so.) Entrepreneurs in particular find it hard to know when to drop back and punt.

Author and historian Arnold Toynbee once said, "To be able to fill leisure intelligently is that last product of civilization." He is right on target; an increasing number of people have problems in this area. In fact, I could go so far as to say that the concept of leisure time is on the rocks. As I discussed in *Breathing Space: Living and Working at a Comfortable Pace in a Sped-Up Society*, it no longer means "total hours minus work hours."

Warning
When you force-fit leisure between barrages of constant frenzy, the quality of your leisure is going to suffer. So, for that matter, are you.

True leisure—where you get to enjoy rewarding activities free from work and preoccupation with work—is absolutely vital.

Do the strains of the work week prompt you to place great emphasis on your weekends and other days off? If you seek to relax but are hounded by pressures, it's hard to get legitimate rest—even when you've got the hours to do so.

Retraining Yourself

Hope springs eternal, and I know that you have the ability to change. When I was in Boston visiting my best friend, Peter Hicks, I saw on his den wall the "diploma" he received in kindergarten. It was there as a kind of joke. I was in the same kindergarten class and had saved mine too. His was fading. Perhaps he had exposed it to the sun. When I mentioned that I still had mine, he asked if I could make a clean copy, and send it to him so he could reconstruct his original.

Back home, while I was looking for the diploma, I also found my first-grade report card. This is one of the lifetime treasures *that you don't chuck*. Not having looked at it for years, I eagerly flipped it open.

In those days (right after dinosaurs ruled the world), report cards came in booklet form. The teachers actually hand-wrote both the letter grade and the comments at the bottom. As I looked at each of the grades, I smiled, "A, B, A, A..." Then I got to arithmetic and saw the "C."

I didn't remember being bad in arithmetic. In fact, I led my high school in SAT scores for math. I looked down at the bottom where the teacher had written, "Jeff has a good understanding of arithmetic fundamentals, but he rushes his work and sometimes makes careless errors." I was aghast. Here I was, decades later, still making the same kinds of errors!

I resolved then and there to be more methodical in my work, whether it related to numbers, writing, or speaking. And I can report that since that time, I have become much more astute.

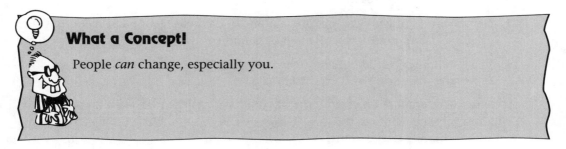

What a Concept!

People *can* change, especially you.

In late 1989, I sent a book proposal to an editor at Warner Books for a book titled *A Layman's Guide for Saving the Planet*. This book would tell readers how they could walk through their homes, room by room, and be more environmentally responsible. The editor sent me back a rejection letter saying he thought the proposal and book had great merit, but the editorial staff at Warner felt that no one in America realistically would change their "cozy, comfortable lifestyles."

Four months later, another publisher released the book, *50 Simple Things You Can Do to Save the Earth*. It quickly became a worldwide best-seller, endorsed at the highest levels of business and government, including the White House. Several other environmental books quickly followed, many of them doing quite well.

Since then many organizations, including state and local governments, have initiated environmentally sound policies. Many recycling centers were created. People began to recognize the value of recycling newspapers, tin cans, plastic, and other materials. It turns out the editors at Warner were wrong. People can change. You can change.

Here are some suggestions for periodically abandoning the rat race, starting with small steps:

1. Give yourself permission to go a whole weekend without reading anything, as mentioned in Chapter 18.

2. Decide to put your home phone answering machine on "answer," flip the ringer off, and don't play back any messages until the next day.

3. Collect all the magazines piling up around your house and give them away—to a retirement community, library, or school.

4. Go ahead and schedule that spa treatment you've been dying to take.

5. Make an agreement to exchange photos with a friend you haven't seen in years. Mail your friend two or three photos of you and the family, and receive two or three in return, or spend one Sunday afternoon writing or calling friends and relatives with whom you've lost touch.

6. Unplug your phone each Friday night.

7. Get schedules of your favorite professional or amateur teams, and mark on your calendar the appropriate dates to sit back and enjoy the games.

8. Visit a botanical garden to enjoy the variety of flowers; let your sense of smell, rather than your eyes and ears, dominate.

9. Attend the graduation ceremonies of your local high school, even if you don't know anyone who's graduating. Recapture the spirit of what it's like to complete an important passage in life.

10. Next time you're at the grocery store, pick up a bouquet of fresh flowers and display them somewhere in your home.

11. Walk around your yard barefoot the way you did when you were a kid. Feel the grass between your toes. Stick your feet in dirt or in a puddle.

12. Visit an historical monument and let yourself become immersed in the challenges that people of that era faced.

13. Attend a free lecture some evening about a topic outside your professional interests.

14. Sleep late.

New References

In one of his monthly "power talks," infomercial king and best-selling author Tony Robbins explains why it's important for you to constantly get *new references* in your life. Robbins explains how people can easily fall into the same routines, travel to work the same way, and believe that the world is exactly the way they see it. He suggests getting what he calls "new references" in your life. The new references come from "field trips" you can take yourself—such as going to a small museum, seniors' home, circus, dairy farm, soup kitchen, daycare center, municipal court, open-air market, or any other place you find intriguing, inviting, or awaiting your help.

These references give you a different perspective on the world, and ultimately on your own life. All of them represent small steps—it's not like I'm asking you to take a week away from your job or go hiking in the Himalayas.

What new references will you incorporate in the next week or month?

Recharging Yourself

The value of periodically abandoning the rat race, or your personal rat race, is that it gives you the opportunity to recharge yourself. Remember from Chapter 7 (on the value of getting more sleep) what it would be like if you could recharge yourself like a rechargeable battery? If you could have that old zip and zest or a twinkle in your eye when you came in to work? If you could have the stamina to put in a full workday, but still leave with lots of energy?

Johnny Carson's *last* guests were Robin Williams and Bette Midler. Why these two people of the thousands of possibilities? Many actors and actresses, comedians, and other types of entertainers would have given their eyeteeth to be on this celebrated show which attracted tens of millions of viewers. I brought this question up with friends; after tossing about several possibilities, we came up with what has to be the answer:

Warning
How can you possibly exude high energy if you plow ahead day after day at the same old grind, short-changing your sleep, short-changing your rest, and perhaps never taking any true vacations?

➤ Robin Williams was about the highest-energy male Johnny Carson could have had as a guest.

➤ Bette Midler was about the highest-energy female Johnny Carson could have had as a guest.

Both performers exude energy. As a showman, Johnny Carson learned quickly that what you offer to your audience *is* energy. So it is with you and your career. What you offer to your employer, employees, customers, or coworkers is energy.

What a Concept!

The more positive energy you offer, the greater your returns in terms of the wages you earn, the business you generate, or the synergy you achieve.

How can you recharge yourself and rev up your energy level, if you're not willing to occasionally drop back and punt? Do you think Robin Williams, Steve Martin, or any other *seemingly* manic comedian, can charge ahead at full throttle all the time? No way.

No Phone, No Media, No Noise

"Fifty Days Away"—that's what Joe Kita, a writer for *Men's Health* magazine, took recently to recharge and renew himself (it's also the title of his article about the experience in the March 1995 issue). Kita feels that even if you get three or four weeks of paid vacation a year, you're probably finding it difficult to take merely five consecutive days off. He arranged his life so that he could take *50 days* away from work. He found that this "near-retirement experience" enlightened him in a way that didn't typically happen during one or even two-week vacations. Here's a summary of what happened:

1. **He started dreaming again.** After a few days away he was having incredible dreams, as if he was directing major motion pictures. He found it amazing that all that dream activity was somehow quite restful. He'd wake feeling fresh and alive. During this time he learned that everyone dreams every night. When you get highly restful sleep, *and as much as you need*, your dream-rich REM periods last longer; you wake up feeling more refreshed.

2. **He lost track of time.** With little reason to look at the clock, or even at the calendar, time began to slow down. Kita said he felt like a kid again. After years of seeing his life speed by almost without control, the days began to pass at a gentler pace. He walked, rather than drove, to the store.

3. **His memory returned.** Being saturated with so much information had a dampening effect on his memory. He remarked that people today are bombarded with more daily intelligence than J. Edgar Hoover ever encountered. When the shelling subsides, even for a short period of time, your memory can spring back in full bloom.

4. **He became more thoughtful.** Kita recalls during his hectic working time, that he never truly read anything, he scanned. He never saw anything, he glanced. During his time away from the rat race he began to chew his food and digest it properly. He even began to taste it.

5. **He became calmer.** He began to notice that he was more patient with his children. He was able to listen to his wife. He found that, in general, he was more tolerant in dealing with others.

6. **He was able to re-divert energy.** He discovered what amazing things he could accomplish with a little time off. He painted his entire house, analyzed and restructured all his investments, and even cleaned out his T-shirt drawer.

7. **He gained new perspective.** He began to see that few jobs in this world carry life-or-death consequences. He discovered that it's productive to be unproductive sometimes. He gave up feeling guilty about occasionally doing nothing.

8. **He rediscovered sex.** The biggest obstacles to the sex lives of working men, said Kita, were not enough time, and fatigue. Since he had enough time now—and wasn't tired—his libido returned. Such a life.

Are there any downsides to staying away from work? Yes—you might lose a bit of your self-worth. If you're a man, what you do at work is often tied to who you are as a person (perhaps this is a little less so for women). Predictably, you may start looking forward to going back to work. After all, you chose your work and remain at it (at least I hope you do) because you're good at it and well suited to it. You get strokes from it as well as income.

How to Have a Leisure Seizure

When you feel ready to live life at a more leisurely pace, whether or not you're taking time off from work, signs appear. You wake naturally without an alarm clock—and have time to reflect each morning. If it is a workday, you leave the office on time at the end of the day, engrossed with what you'll do next, without any thoughts of work.

If you're ready to drop back and punt, but aren't quite ready to take a huge chunk of time away from work, here are some things you can do right where you are to ease the throttle back on the pace of your life:

➤ Play with your child for hours on a Saturday afternoon without any concern for time.

➤ Eat dinner early in the evening, and have time to take a stroll or whatever you feel like doing.

➤ Resubscribe to the local community theater's fall series—and actually attend.

➤ Re-engage in one of your hobbies (as discussed in Chapter 18) with renewed enthusiasm.

➤ Make a new friend about once a month. From where? Who knows? They start showing up because you've allowed time for it to happen.

➤ Book a cruise or cross-continental trip, maybe for the first time, or the first time in years.

➤ Volunteer for a charitable or civic activity in which you've long wanted to help, but until now have not taken action to help.

➤ View a sunrise at least once a month, and maybe even once a week. Also, view many, many sunsets each month.

➤ Frequent some of the area's best parks. Occasionally feed the ducks.

Ten Ways to Know When You Need to Drop Back and Punt

As the chapter comes to a close, here's a list, in ascending order, of indications that you have let things slide a tad too long (and had better reread this chapter closely):

10. You believe that Michael Jordan is currently employed someplace in the Chicago White Sox organization.

9. You know that Margaret Thatcher is no longer prime minister of Great Britain, but you haven't found out who is.

8. You're not sure what "Forrest Gump" means. You think it's some type of growth at the foot of a tree.

7. You recently drove to the local "record store" only to find that they no longer sell records.

6. You're on the last notch of your favorite belt, and it's still way too tight.

5. You're looking forward to going to your tenth high school reunion, when you realize it's actually your fifteenth (or twentieth!).

4. You're not only eating lunch at your desk, you're starting to eat dinner at your desk.

3. Your boss keeps asking you to take a vacation.

2. Your wallet is twice as thick as your index finger.

1. Your kid sees you walking up your sidewalk and asks, "Can I help you, sir?"

The Least You Need to Know

➤ No matter what hours you've put in over the last several years, you can retrain yourself to approach your work and time in more rewarding ways.

➤ Everyone needs to recharge themselves, especially you. When you're recharged, you have more energy; all your relationships go better.

➤ You need a vacation. Start planning a real one now.

➤ There are many small steps you can initiate, even before taking time away from work, to achieve a more leisurely pace—such as playing with your child for hours on a Saturday or subscribing to the local community theater series.

The Best Is Yet to Come

Whether you're 28, 38, 48, or somewhere in-between, it's time to start looking at your life as if the best years are yet to come, for indeed they can be coming. Sure, you'll get a little slower with each advancing year, but you have the ability to put together all that you've learned in each decade (this is sometimes referred to as wisdom). Perhaps you'll be even more prudent with your time. More than 100 years ago, in his essay of "The Feeling of Immortality and Youth," British essayist William Hazlitt said, "As we advance in life, we acquire a keener sense of the value of time. Nothing else, indeed, seems of any consequence, and we become misers in this respect." That may be true, yet as you learned in Chapter 2, you probably have more time left on this planet than you think.

Life is a Marathon...Not a Sprint!

Regardless of how old you are, or how much time you have left, anytime is a good time to practice measures for winning back your time. You may even find it rewarding to revel in your current age—it holds so much potential. Marlee Matlin won the Academy Award for Best Actress at age 21; Jessica Tandy won it at age 80. The U.S. Constitution was written by men who were, on average, 40 years of age—when the *life expectancy* was barely 40. Sure, there were some old-timers like Ben Franklin, but most of the founding fathers were young by today's standards.

What a Concept!

The key to accepting your age and your life is to realize that people shift into high gear at different times. It's hard to predict who's going to take off when.

James Michener didn't write his first novel until age 42. Forty-two years later, he's still writing best-sellers. As I hit the big four-oh, I started to feel a little uncomfortable about the passing time in my life. Now, as I'm closer to 50, for some reason I feel more at ease about how I use my time. I found it comforting to look up the birthdates of notable people who were about the same age as I am:

02/22/50 Julius Erving

01/09/51 Crystal Gayle

01/09/51 Stevie Wonder

01/12/51 Rush Limbaugh

01/13/51 Jeff Davidson!

01/30/51 Phil Collins

02/15/51 Melissa Manchester

02/15/51 Jane Seymour

04/10/51 Steven Seagal

07/05/51 Huey Lewis

07/08/51 Angelica Houston

09/09/51   Michael Keaton

10/07/51   John Cougar

05/01/52   Mr. T

06/07/52   Liam Neeson

When Elvis was my age, he'd been dead for three years! (Unless, of course, you've sighted him recently...) Some people take up marathon running in their fifties. Some people take it up in their sixties. Become comfortable with your current age, and recognize the vast potential you have with all your remaining years. Alice Cornyn-Selby, a prolific author and speaker from Portland, Oregon, uses two powerful key phrases with her audiences:

1. "I have now come to the end of my life and I'm disappointed that I didn't...."

   How did you finish that sentence? Whatever you thought, whatever came up first, is probably something you want to do right away. No use putting it off any longer, since it bubbled up to the surface immediately.

2. "I have now come to the end of my life and I'm glad that I...."

   What did you come up with this time? Was it the same issue that you addressed in the first statement? Was it something you've already accomplished? When you begin to look at the opportunities that await, and those you can create, all the rushing about that came before and the times you felt you were missing your life can begin to melt away—as you head in the direction that will give you deep satisfaction.

Completions to This Moment

As you learned in Chapter 15, the more often you can feel complete about your accomplishments, the more energy, focus, and direction you'll have. All things end, whether poorly or wonderfully. Tasks, whether they take a few seconds or an astronomical epoch, have ending points.

➤ 100-watt light bulb's life	750 hours
➤ Columbus's first 1492 trip	70 days
➤ Car muffler	2.5 years
➤ Car water pump	3.5 years
➤ U.S. presidential term	4.0 years
➤ Skylab's time in orbit	6.2 years

➤ A year on Jupiter	11.9 years
➤ The Cold War	43.5 years
➤ The Soviet Union	61.9 years
➤ Your life	??? years
➤ Human organs	115 years
➤ The 100 Years War	116 years
➤ The Crusades	196 years
➤ The Holy Roman Empire	841 years
➤ Cro-Magnon Man	30,000 years
➤ The Jurassic Period	64,000,000 years
➤ Dinosaurs (Mesozoic Era)	165,000,000 years
➤ Earth before *homo erectus*	4,000,000,000 years
➤ Sun's remaining life	5,000,000,000 years

You can use completion-thinking to get "caught up" with this moment, feel good about everything that's transpired thus far, and be energized for what's ahead. In The Fountain of Age, Betty Friedan closes with a remarkable paragraph:

"I am myself at this age. It took me these years to put the missing pieces together, to confront my own age in terms of integrity, and generativity, moving into the unknown future with a comfort now, instead of being stuck in the past. I have never felt so free."

New Kinds of Goals

Now then, what kind of completions can you realize about your own life? What kind of goals do you want to make, given the fact that today represents a new opportunity to reclaim your life? Not like that trite old phrase, "Today's the first day in the rest of your life," but with a deeper realization that you can be in control.

Following is a set of new goals you might want to entertain. These aren't ones that traditionally make achievers' lists, but they can be important to the quality of your life.

1. **Weight.** What weight do you want to be one year from now or five years from now? Or, what size waistline do you want to have? Do you want to become as fit as you've been at other times? It's possible, but it's a choice you'll have to make first.

2. **Blood pressure.** I'll bet you never thought of this. Would you like to get your blood pressure down to 120 over 80? What foods and habits are you willing to give up to accomplish this, to keep your blood pressure at a safe, healthy level?

3. **Resting pulse per minute.** How hard is your heart working for you right now? Is your resting pulse above 80? You should know that 70 beats per minute, and even 60, are quite possible. My average is 52. I know a 65-year-old who averages 42.

   Hold on, before you think the guy must be about to keel over, look at it from a physiological standpoint: his heart is working efficiently. In the course of a day, a week, or a year, it's beating far less than yours. He is this way by ensuring that each day he takes walks that last between 15 minutes and an hour.

4. **Hours of sleep nightly.** You know by now the paramount importance of sleep. One year or five years from now, how much do you want to be sleeping each night? It's up to you.

5. **Healthy foods regularly consumed.** You may not be able to eat the recommended three to five helpings of vegetables each day, or the two to three helpings of fruit, but you could probably add a lot more of both to your diet. You don't have to visit a health store to eat healthily. You only have to choose fresh foods from your traditional supermarket.

6. **Vitamins taken regularly.** If you're over thirty, this grows in importance each day. Do you take a multi-vitamin? Do you take specific vitamins throughout the day to ensure peak performance? If you're in a highly stressful position, you probably need a good B-complex vitamin. Maybe you're not getting enough vitamin C. When's the last time you visited a nutritionist or dietitian, and figured out what supplements would be best, given your lifestyle and physiology?

7. **Great novels read.** To make the best yet to come, you can have goals beyond simply health and fitness. What great novels would you like to read, but year after year haven't begun? One option is that today most great novels are on cassette. Perhaps listening to them, rather than reading them, is your cup of tea. Either way, the choice—and the ability to get started—is yours. (Hint: Children love to be read to; it can be a rejuvenating treat for adults.)

8. **Classic or inspiring movies viewed.** Sure, it's easy enough to go down to the video store and rent the latest shoot-'em-up or chase-scene movie. Instead, what about a good biographical video? Or how about an historical novel on video? What about a documentary? At any given moment, you have a lot of alternatives in terms of what you're viewing.

What a Concept!

If you want to improve the quality of your life for the rest of your life, you can start with what you take out of the video store on your next trip.

9. **Family involvement.** Perhaps you're already good at this, but perhaps it's an area to revisit. Have you been to your son's Boy Scout troop meeting lately? Have you ever watched your daughter for a full soccer practice? Have you had a real family outing—not the kind where you go to a theme park, spend money, and have hectic fun, but where you bring a picnic basket, hike together, talk to each other, and spend the day in a quiet and enjoyable way?

The World Will Become More Complex

As you learned in Chapters 2 and 11, population information, media growth, too much paper, and an over-abundance of choices, all converge to make it feel as if you have never had enough time. Realistically, these factors will be heightened in the next decade.

You can count on complexity increasing. I see three possible scenarios: (1) Few people learn how to win back their time; (2) Some people learn how to win back their time; or (3) Most people learn how to win back their time.

1. *Few people* **learn how to win back their time.** What will society look like under this scenario? In the social environment there will continue to be high stress, constant breakdowns, perhaps neglect of children, people walking around in an overwhelmed state. In this scenario more catastrophes will occur: train wrecks, plane crashes, auto mishaps.

   In the business environment, you will see more stress and burnout among professionals, increasing hostility, more people walking around in microsleep. You will also see more cluttered desks and more people constantly playing catch-up. What's the typical, individual response in a society where everybody is on fast-forward and no one is in control of his or her time? More "me-first" attitudes, more investment in creature comforts that don't truly comfort, more feelings of disenfranchisement. Not pleasant.

2. *Some people* **win back control of their time.** In the social environment feeling overwhelmed is only intermittent. Breakdowns are seen as routine, but at least they're not constant.

In the business environment, management training can alleviate some of the problems. What is the typical, individual response to being in a world where only some people are in control of their time (much like today)? Such people will choose fewer projects, but they'll be more important ones. They will be a little less stressed out because they understand what's going on. They'll try to find more enjoyment in leisure, and clear their weekends free of work.

Go!
Bad bosses, bad organizations, the whole world itself in a frenzy—none of these need diminish your enjoyment and quality of life. It's all a matter of choice.

3. *Most people* **win back their time.** In the social environment, under such a favorable scenario, there will be a strong concentration on the family. More individuals will exhibit balance and control. There will even be a further development of the social graces.

   In the business environment people will be able to have vacations and leisure time available on request. Businesses will stay lean, but only *mean* to the competition; managers, from the top CEO down to line supervisors, will be able to display confidence and compassion. They'll be able to respond to the requests and concerns of their employees—*people* will be of primary importance. Wages will actually increase. Efficiency and effectiveness will be the name of the game.

   What is the typical individual's response to existing in an environment where most people have control of their time? A "we-first" orientation is maintained amidst a quest for personal betterment. The individual pursues cultural as well as social endeavors, keeping an astute eye on the environment.

You can prevail under any scenario. Regardless of which scenario comes to pass, your ability to win back your time is up to you.

Choices, Choices

You can make choices, of course, about any aspect of your time and life, be it issues of work, change, technology, success, travel, health and well-being, relationships, marriage, or parenting.

Abundant research shows that after 21 days of repeating an affirmation to yourself, notable positive change occurs. Why? Your subconscious mind accepts the statements you give it repeatedly; it can't discern between what exists now and what you've chosen for your future! (Generally the people who don't credit the power of affirmations have never used and trusted the process.)

As with any quest to reinforce the choices you make, write or type your decisions and post them, or record them on cassette and play them back. How many choices can you make in a sitting. There is no limit, although I'd suggest making no more than a dozen. Choose what feels right, and keep choosing. While you're waiting in a bank line, run through your choices. If you notice yourself wavering, recall the new behavior or feeling that you've chosen.

Some profound choices you can make are listed next. Read them all and circle the ones that best meet your present needs. You may want to craft your own choices, using your own words. Keep reminding yourself of them *for at least 21 days*.

Aging and Well-Being

➤ I choose to feel good about the age I am and relish the years I have left.

➤ I choose to face the future with confidence.

➤ I choose to adopt a healthy lifestyle.

Career Changes

➤ I choose to feel good about my career move.

➤ I choose to be open to new ideas and information.

➤ I choose to apply the lessons from previous careers effectively in my new career.

Change in General

➤ I choose to handle change with grace and ease.

➤ I choose to thrive on challenging situations.

➤ I choose to master changing technology in my field.

The Future

➤ I choose to acknowledge that things will work out for the best.

➤ I choose to face the future boldly and decisively.

➤ I choose to arise each morning with great anticipation.

Opportunity

➤ I choose to recognize and create opportunities.

➤ I choose to see each minute as new.

➤ I choose to be open to new avenues for prosperity.

Personal Development

➤ I choose to be an active listener.

➤ I choose to personify grace and ease.

➤ I choose to acknowledge others often.

I find affirmations like these useful as *starting points*, especially when you are trying out a new idea that has always seemed out of reach before. To help fulfill an affirmation, ask yourself at the end of the 21 days, "What specific *actions* have I taken to follow through on this choice I have made?" Write down three specific instances.

The Choice of Choices

An essential choice in life is choosing to feel worthy and complete. This helps me to reduce anxiety, stay calm, and feel more relaxed. I learned this choice from Pat McCallum, author of *Essence Repatterning*. Depending on how long it's been since you've felt worthy and complete, you may have to reaffirm this choice for many days or weeks running. Nevertheless, keep at it.

What a Concept!

By choosing *to feel worthy and complete*, you automatically help redirect yourself and begin to accept that there is nothing you "must" do. Everything is based on your choice.

If you choose to continue working on some task, even one assigned to you, you make that choice in the present moment, not in response to a prior agenda. A worthy and complete feeling yields a sense of inner harmony.

The Least You Need to Know

➤ The factors that have conspired to make you feel time-pressed are likely to only intensify in the coming years.

➤ While you'll get older, and perhaps become a little slower, the best is yet to come, because you'll be able to draw upon your wisdom to steer your life faithfully in the desired direction.

➤ You can choose to see the totality and completions of your life up to this minute, anytime you want.

➤ Whenever you desire, you can make fundamental choices about how you want your life to go.

➤ The fundamental choices you can make regarding your time are, "I choose to feel good about how I spend my time," and, "I choose to easily have all the time I need to accomplish my goals and lead a balanced life."

➤ Follow through!

Bibliography

Biggs, Dick, *If Life Is a Balancing Act, Why Am I So Darn Clumsy?* (Chattahoochee Press, 1993).

Choate, Pat, *Agents of Influence* (Knopf, 1990).

Csikszentmihalyi, Mihaly, *Flow: The Psychology of Optimal Experience* (Harper, 1990).

Davidson, Jeff, *Breathing Space: Living and Working at a Comfortable Pace in a Sped-Up Society* (MasterMedia, 1991).

Davidson, Jeff, *Marketing on a Shoestring* (Wiley, 1994).

Dychtwald, Ken, Ph.D., *Age Wave* (Tarcher, 1989).

Fisher, Jeffrey A., M.D., *RX 2000: Breakthroughs in Health, Medicine and Longevity by the Year 2000 and Beyond* (Simon & Schuster, 1994).

Friedan, Betty, *The Fountain of Age* (Simon & Schuster, 1993).

Fritz, Robert, *The Path of Least Resistance* (Fawcett Columbine, 1989).

Grant, Lindsey, ed., *Elephants in the Volkswagen* (W. H. Freeman, 1991).

Jeffers, Susan, *Feel the Fear and Do It Anyway* (Harcourt, Brace & Jovanovich, 1987).

Johnson, Magic, *My Life* (Random House, 1992).

McCallum, Pat, *Essence Repatterning* (Choice Publications, 1993).

Minkin, Barry Howard, *EconoQuake* (Prentice-Hall, 1993).

Moore-Ede, Martin, M.D., Ph.D., *The 24-Hour Society* (Addison-Wesley, 1993).

Postman, Neil, Ph.D., *Amusing Ourselves to Death* (Viking, 1985).

Postman, Neil, Ph.D., *Technopoly* (Knopf, 1992).

Rajineesh, Osho, *Don't Just Do Something, Sit There* (Maineesha 1980).

Rose, Kenneth, *The Organic Clock* (Wiley, 1988).

Schor, Judith, *Consumerism* (Basic Books, 1993).

Shenkman, Richard, *Legends, Lies, and Cherished Myths of American History* (William Morrow Books, 1989).

Toffler, Alvin, *Future Shock* (Random House, 1970).

Twitchell, James, *Carnival Culture* (Columbia University Press, 1992).

Wagner, Ronald L., and Engelmann, Eric, *The McGraw-Hill Internet Training Guide* (McGraw-Hill, 1996).

Waitely, Denis, *Timing is Everything* (Pocket Books, 1993).

Wills, Christopher, *The Run Away Brain: The Evolution of Human Uniqueness* (Harper Collins, 1993).

Articles

"In the Presence of Animals: Health Professionals No Longer Scoff at the Therapeutic Effects of Pets." *U.S. News & World Report*, February 24, 1992.

Index